The Meaning of Nolan Ryan

The Meaning of
NOLAN RYAN
By Nick Trujillo

TEXAS A&M UNIVERSITY PRESS : COLLEGE STATION

B
RYAN

Library of Congress Cataloging-in-Publication Data

Trujillo, Nick, 1955–
    The meaning of Nolan Ryan / by Nick Trujillo. – 1st ed.
        p.   cm.
    Includes bibliographical references (p.   ) and index.
    ISBN 0-89096-574-9. – ISBN 0-89096-575-7 (pbk.)
        1. Ryan, Nolan, 1947– .   2. Baseball players–United States–
Biography.   3. Hero worship–United States.   I. Title.
GV865.R9T78   1994
796.357'092–dc20
    [B]   93-28038
                                                                  CIP

Contents

Preface

In the summer of 1972, I was a sixteen-year-old pitcher for my American Legion baseball team in Las Vegas, Nevada. That summer our team traveled to Southern California to play a variety of American Legion teams in the Los Angeles area. We won a few games, and we lost a few games. But the highlight of the trip was going to Anaheim Stadium to see Nolan Ryan pitch in his first season as a California Angel.

Everyone on the team had heard of Nolan Ryan. And all of us, especially the pitchers, were quite excited about the prospect of seeing him pitch. When we saw him throw that first fastball, we were simply in awe. How could anyone throw the ball that hard?

I don't remember the outcome of the game, but I do remember that Ryan struck out about a dozen batters and walked another seven or eight. It seemed like a typical Nolan Ryan outing. I also remember that on the three hundred-mile return trip to Las Vegas, we talked a lot about how hard Nolan Ryan threw the baseball.

I went on to have a relatively uneventful baseball career at the University of Southern California as a 5'11" right-handed pitcher. Although Marcel Lachemann, my pitching coach, told me that I had a "major league slider," I knew that I had a minor league fastball. I didn't get in too many innings my senior year, and instead of pursuing baseball after graduation, I went to graduate school. Somewhat bitter about my USC experiences, I forgot about baseball for several years as I finished my master's and Ph.D. degrees in communication, and as I taught and did research during my first professorship at Purdue University.

My interest in baseball rekindled a few years later when I took a job at Southern Methodist University in Dallas, Texas, a city with a major league team. After finishing a study on how organizations are portrayed on prime-time television, I decided to return to baseball, this time as a researcher, to do a study of a major league baseball franchise.

I called up the Texas Rangers, the local franchise, and made appointments to speak with the president, Mike Stone, and with the general manager, Tom Grieve. Both men were informative, helpful, and friendly, and they suggested that I also speak with a variety of other managers and supervisors in the Rangers' organization. Soon thereafter, I was meeting with members of the franchise virtually every week.

I received formal permission to study the franchise before the 1988 season. I was not interested in studying major league ballplayers, per se, because I wanted to study the broader "culture" of the ballpark through the eyes of people who worked there—from the owners and executives who sat in suites, to the middle managers who ran stadium operations and security, to the part-timers who sold peanuts and directed cars in the parking lot. I found the ballpark to be a fascinating culture, and at the end of the 1988 season, I received permission to continue the study into 1989.

In December 1988, however, the Ranger franchise did something unexpected: it signed free agent and Texas native Nolan Ryan. News of the signing spread quickly in the Ranger franchise and throughout the Dallas-Fort Worth area. The ticket office received nonstop calls from people wanting to buy season tickets. Company executives who had turned down advertisements in game programs and sponsorship of promotions changed their minds and adjusted their budgets. The number of people applying for part-time positions as ushers, vendors, and parking lot attendants rose dramatically. Newspaper, radio, and television reports discussed Ryan's potential impact on the team and on the entire community's economy.

Everyone in the franchise knew immediately that the 1989 season would be a very different one. And I promised myself that I would not only study the ballpark workers, but also how Nolan Ryan affected them.

The 1989 season was indeed special. Ryan's debut as a Ranger drew a record crowd for a second game. (Veteran Ranger pitcher Charlie Hough pitched on opening night.) Ryan had some classic matchups, none more riveting than his 2-1 win over Roger Clemens at the end of April. He struck out Bo Jackson the first several times he faced him, but then Bo got even when he launched a line drive home run over the center field fence, silencing the crowd at Arlington Stadium.

Then, in August, after the Rangers had played themselves out of contention, Ryan registered his five thousandth strikeout against Rickie Henderson of the Oakland Athletics. The media was in a frenzy at the event, as more than two hundred reporters squeezed their way into every seam of the ballpark. The crowd was electrified, popping thousands of camera flash bulbs on every two-strike pitch after Ryan had registered number 4,999. The atmosphere in the ballpark that night was more exciting than at a World Series game. The season was filled with moments like these.

I continued to study the Ranger franchise and Nolan Ryan at the start of the 1990 season, but I moved to California in July to take a job at

California State University in Sacramento. My wife and I were driving
to California on July 31st as Ryan started pitching against the Milwaukee
Brewers, going for his 300th victory. The radio faded in and out all night
as we searched for stations carrying the game near Amarillo, Tucumcari,
Santa Rosa, and other desert towns. We pulled off the interstate near
Albuquerque and celebrated with a kiss as the last out was made and
Ryan joined the 300-win club.

While living in California the last few years, I have come to appreciate
that admiration of Nolan Ryan is not just a Texas phenomenon. I was
amazed when Ryan's picture was put on the front page of the *Sacramento
Bee* on May 2, 1991, the day after his seventh no-hitter, while the same
day virtual hometown hero Rickie Henderson's picture was relegated to
the sports page after he broke Lou Brock's all-time stolen base record. Seeing Nolan Ryan as a national phenomenon led me to study the media
coverage of his career and to write this book.

In a sense, a book is never really the sole product of a single author,
and many people helped me along the way to finishing this one. I would
like to thank many current and former members of the Texas Rangers
franchise, especially Mike Stone, Tom Grieve, George W. Bush, Mat Stolley,
John Blake, Larry Kelly, Bobby Bragan, Dave Fendrick, Chuck Morgan,
Barry Worden, Chuck Wangner, John McMichael, Jay Miller, Taunee Paur,
Bob Garvey, Joe Macko, Monte Clegg, Della Britton, John Welaj, Jeannie
Wangner, and the countless full-timers and part-timers who shared their
stories with me at the ballpark. This book is dedicated to them.

Several others helped in the formulation and preparation of this book.
My colleagues from the annual Cooperstown Symposium on Baseball and
American Culture, where I presented a paper titled "The Meaning of Nolan
Ryan" in 1990, offered many comments about the work (especially my good
friend Richard Gaughran). Tom Heitz and Bill Deane and the rest of the
staff at the National Baseball Library in Cooperstown were helpful in providing material from their Nolan Ryan files. The people at Texas A&M
University Press were very supportive of the project, especially Noel Par-
sons, who offered continuous encouragement. Dick Costa, who reviewed
the manuscript for the Press, gave early drafts a fine and thorough going-
over.

I am grateful to the publishers and copyright holders for permission
to reprint written material for this book which appeared earlier in the
following sources: "From Wild Western Prodigy to the Ageless Wonder:
The Mediated Evolution of Nolan Ryan" (written with Leah R. Vande
Berg), in *American Heroes in the Media Age*, edited by Robert Cathcart
and Gary Gumpert, reprinted with permission of Hampton Press, Inc.,
copyright 1993; "The Meaning of Nolan Ryan," in *Cooperstown Symposium
on Baseball and the American Culture, 1990*, edited by Alvin L. Hall, re-

printed with permission of Meckler Publishing, copyright 1991; and "Hegemonic Masculinity on the Mound: Media Representations of Nolan Ryan and American Sports Culture," in *Critical Studies in Mass Communication* 8 (3), reprinted with permission of the Speech Communication Association, copyright 1991.

My good friend and colleague Harry Haines of Trinity University suggested that I consider Ryan as a symbol of masculinity, perhaps the most provocative idea in the book. I also thank my friend Howard Green, the former president of the Ex-Pro Ballplayers of Texas and the current president of the Dallas-Fort Worth chapter of the Society for American Baseball Research, who shared his thoughts with me from time to time at the ballpark.

On a personal note, I thank my parents, Bill and Claudia Trujillo, who offered continuous support through the ups and downs of my baseball career in Little League, Midget League, Colt League, American Legion, high school, and college. My colleague, friend, and spouse, Leah Vande Berg, also a professor at California State University at Sacramento, supported me in so many ways, especially as I scrambled to meet various deadlines.

Finally, I thank Nolan Ryan. Though I have shaken his hand a couple times at Ranger banquets and have hung an autographed poster of him above my computer at home, I cannot say that I know him personally. But like most baseball fans in America, I have come to know him through the mass media. I don't know if Ryan will like this book, especially the more critical chapters on his status as a commodity and as a "safe sex symbol," but he should know that this book ultimately stands as a tribute to his meaning in American culture.

The Meaning of Nolan Ryan

Introduction

Seven no-hitters. Over three hundred wins. Over fifty-five hundred strikeouts. Over five thousand innings pitched. Over twenty-six seasons of major league baseball. Over fifty major league records.

Three autobiographies. Feature stories in *Life, Time, Newsweek, Saturday Evening Post, Gentlemen's Quarterly,* and many sports magazines. Commercial endorsements for Advil, Bic shavers, Duracell batteries, Nike, Southwest Airlines, Whataburger, Wrangler Jeans, and others. A stretch of Texas highway renamed the "Ryan Expressway." A Jerry Jeff Walker song titled "Nolan Ryan (He's a Hero to Us All)".

Lynn Nolan Ryan has become a national phenomenon. He is one of the most impressive pitchers in major league history, a player with amazing physical talent and staying power who could throw a baseball at over 90 miles per hour in his mid-forties. He has been called the "ageless wonder," "miracle man," and "one of the last real sports heroes." He has become one of the hottest sports celebrities as well, with a variety of cover stories and commercial endorsements to his credit. Some have even called him a sex symbol because of his clean-cut appearance and his off-the-field job as a rancher. In this book, I examine these and other aspects of Nolan Ryan's meaning in American culture.

One of the Best Pitchers Ever?

Baseball analysts and fans alike now agree that Nolan Ryan is one of the best pitchers ever and that he is a certain first-ballot selection to the Hall of Fame five years after his retirement. But Ryan has slowly earned the respect he now enjoys over his twenty-seven-year career in baseball.

Nolan Ryan made his major league debut as a nineteen-year-old pitcher with the New York Mets on September 11, 1966, when he went two innings against the Atlanta Braves, giving up one earned run on one hit while striking out three and walking one. He made no major league appearances in 1967 as he fulfilled military obligations and struggled with injuries. In 1968 he began the first of twenty-six consecutive seasons in the major leagues with the Mets (1968–71), the California Angels (1972–79), the Houston Astros (1980–88), and the Texas Rangers (1989–93).

Ryan reached many milestones on the field during his remarkable career. Through 1993 he owned or shared more than fifty major league records, including career records for most strikeouts (5,714), most no-hitters (7), most one-hitters (12), most walks (2,795), most wild pitches (277), highest strikeout average per nine innings (9.55), and lowest hits allowed average per nine innings (6.54). He also was the oldest pitcher to win an All-Star game (at forty-two in 1989) and the oldest pitcher to throw a no-hitter (at forty-four in 1991).

For many students of the game, Ryan's strikeout and no-hitter records represent his essential contribution to major league baseball. To attain his fifty-five hundred-plus strikeouts, a pitcher has to average about 225 strikeouts a season for twenty-five years. Only ten pitchers have reached 3,000 strikeouts, and only one, Steven Carlton, ever reached 4,000 (with 4,136). Ryan also has seven no-hitters, two of them coming when he was in his forties. Since 1900 only Sandy Koufax has pitched four no-hitters, and only two players have pitched three (Bob Feller and Jim Maloney). In these two categories, Ryan stands alone on the mound—and in the history books.

For other students of the game, Ryan's three hundred-plus wins represent his importance in baseball history. When Ryan beat the Milwaukee Brewers on July 31, 1990, he became only the twentieth pitcher in history to win 300 games. That victory was a testament to Ryan's longevity, and it secured his place in baseball's Hall of Fame.

Rating Nolan Ryan by the Numbers
"Sabermetricians" (members of SABR, the Society for American Baseball Research) and other baseball analysts have spent much time rating Ryan's success as a major league pitcher. Critics have charged that Ryan was only a mediocre pitcher because his won-lost record hovered just above .500, a criticism that hounded Ryan throughout his lengthy career. But Ryan's defenders have countered that he played for mediocre teams—and that he won more games for these teams than they would have won without him. *The 1991 Elias Baseball Analyst*, for example, revealed that Ryan's own record was better than his team's record in fourteen of the twenty-one seasons in which he had at least fifteen decisions; in fact, for five of those seasons, Ryan's winning percentage was at least 100 percentage points higher than his team's record. The authors concluded with the somewhat

esoteric finding "that a .400 pitcher substituting for Ryan throughout his career would have won 224 games — 78 fewer wins than Ryan's actual total." They also noted that "only 14 pitchers since 1893 have compiled margins greater than Ryan's."[1]

Ryan, however, was rarely described as a great pitcher until very late in his career. Ryan was not included in Lawrence Ritter and Donald Honig's *The 100 Greatest Baseball Players of All Times*, published in 1981. He was rated as only the 322nd best player and the 107th best pitcher by John Thorn and Pete Palmer in their *Hidden Game of Baseball*, published in 1984. And he was rated as the 79th best player in Maury Allen's list of *Baseball's 100*, published in 1981. Indeed, sabermetrics guru Bill James said in 1988, "I may get kicked out of the sabermetricians union for saying this, but it seems to me that we've got to start taking Ryan a little more seriously as a great pitcher."[2]

Ryan fared better in a 1987 book by Eugene McCaffrey and Roger McCaffrey, titled *Players' Choice*, which presented ratings from former and current major league players. Among the 645 players who responded to the McCaffreys' survey, Nolan Ryan was rated as the fourteenth best right-handed pitcher of all time, the second best from 1969–85 (behind Tom Seaver). He was rated as the fifth toughest pitcher the respondents had ever faced (behind Bob Feller, Sandy Koufax, Ernie Blackwell, and Bob Gibson), with the second best fastball (behind Feller) and the ninth best curveball (tied with Juan Marichal). However, Ryan was not among the twenty-one pitchers picked to start the seventh game of a World Series. (Incidentally, in the foreword to the book, then Vice-President George Bush rated Ryan as having the best fastball, followed by Dwight Gooden and Bob Feller).

When Ryan became a member of the elite 300-win club in 1990 and was celebrated in the media as the "miracle man," few critics remained, and even fewer would go on the record with their criticism. But don't be surprised if a few sportswriters refuse to vote to induct Ryan into the Hall of Fame on the first ballot because of his so-called mediocre won-lost record.

More Ryan numbers

Other aspects of Ryan's career have been examined by baseball analysts, who have a fetish for the most esoteric statistics. Perhaps the most complete analysis of Ryan's pitching was conducted by the Astros during Ryan's tenure with Houston. Someone with the Astros counted and categorized every pitch that Ryan threw as a member of the team from 1980 to 1988. The Astros conducted this amazingly detailed performance appraisal to determine whether they were getting their money's worth as Ryan aged into his late thirties and early forties. The results of this analysis are summarized in *Nolan Ryan's Pitcher's Bible*, written by Ryan and former Ranger pitching coach Tom House. In nine seasons with the Astros, Ryan threw 17,309 fastballs at an average velocity of 93.76 MPH, with a range of 90–99 MPH; he threw 6,421 curveballs at an average velocity of 78.30 MPH, with a range of 66–83 MPH; and he threw 7,538 change-ups at an average velocity of 82.30 MPH, with a range of 71–89 MPH. The Astros found little evidence that Ryan's power had diminished appreciably over time: his fastballs decreased only slightly in velocity from an average of 95.1 MPH in 1980 to an average of 93.3 MPH in 1988. Despite evidence that Ryan's performance had not deteriorated, the Astros did not re-sign Ryan after the 1988 season, and he went to the Texas Rangers as a free agent.

Baseball analyst Craig Wright, along with Tom House, evaluated Ryan's longevity statistically, arguing that his ability to pitch for so long was a result of his light workload during his early years with the Mets—a light load about which Ryan himself complained. These authors explained that from age eighteen to twenty-five, Ryan threw a relatively low number of innings (801) and had a low BFS (the number of batters faced per start). They showed that among exceptional pitchers who were also durable, Ryan had the most innings as a teenager (205) but had a low BFS of 27.5. Taking into account Ryan's physique and conditioning, they concluded that "what really stands out about Nolan's career is the light workload of his early years."[3]

Bill James estimated the probability of throwing a no-hitter and, somewhat surprisingly, argued that the "most probable" no-hitter ever was Ryan's gem against the Toronto Blue Jays in 1991 when he was forty-four years old. James wrote that the chance of a no-hitter depends on the season batting average against the pitcher, the season batting average of the opposing team, and the season batting average of the league. He estimated that Ryan's no-hitter in 1991 was the "most probable" because Ryan had allowed just 102 hits in 164 innings that year (not including the no-hitter), and the Blue Jays' team batting average was three points below the league average. James concluded by joking, "I figure in five years Ryan will be throwing a no-hitter every third start."[4]

Statistics buffs will continue to analyze every nuance of Ryan's career well into his years as an Equitable Old-Timer (when he will be throwing only in the mid-80 MPH range). It is safe to predict that sabermetricians could wind up spending more years off the field analyzing Ryan's statistical accomplishments than Ryan himself spent on the field achieving them.

Nolan Ryan's meaning transcends the baseball field and the record books. The people who know him personally say that Nolan Ryan is a very special individual. Residents of his hometown of Alvin, Texas, say that Ryan is a "regular guy" who just happens to have nearby roads, parks, museums, and historical societies named after him. Several former and current teammates say he was so inspirational that they named children after him.

Members of the organizations where he played say that Ryan has been a legitimate franchise hero: the California Angels retired his number in 1992, even though he had not played for them since 1979, and the Texas Rangers used to hang a huge poster of him above the entrance to Arlington Stadium as a tribute.

Nolan Ryan also has special meaning to millions of baseball fans across the country. But these fans, even those who have seen him pitch or have obtained his autograph, do not really know Ryan personally. Rather, they have come to "know" Ryan through the mass media.

Sports and the Mass Media

The relationship between professional sports and the mass media in American society has been characterized as a "symbiotic" one, in which sports and media organizations have offered mutual support and experienced complementary growth. Baseball historians, for example, have shown that baseball and the mass media literally grew up together in the mid-nineteenth century. "Matching the dynamic growth of baseball's first dimension," wrote David Voigt, "was the second dimension—the game as played in the daily newspaper." Steven Riess argued that baseball attained success with help from the media not only in the stories about games and players, but also in the "ideology developed by cooperative sports writers which made the sport appear directly relevant to the needs and aspirations of middle America." More recently, media organizations have contributed richly to the bottom lines of sports leagues, teams, and players by signing incredible contracts for the rights to broadcast games.[5]

Media organizations also have enjoyed success due, in large part, to professional sports. For better *and* for worse, many readers still subscribe to daily newspapers just to read the morning sports section. Sports programming remains a vital key to the market positioning of the big three networks, cable channels, and local programming. One report estimated that in the late 1980s, sports in general accounted for over eighteen hundred hours of network television, about five thousand hours of cable television, and countless thousands of hours on local television and radio. The same report pointed out that baseball in particular has enjoyed broadcast coverage of most of the twenty-two hundred pre-season, season, and post-season games each year on radio and on network, cable, and local television. The marriage between professional sports and the mass media is sometimes a rocky one in which, as David Klatell and Norman Marcus put it, "mutual back-scratching occasionally draws blood." Still, the relationship has produced substantial dowries for both parties.[6]

Sports, and media coverage of sports, have changed dramatically over time. Most observers agree that television caused the greatest changes in sports and sports coverage. Critics have charged that television and base-ball executives contaminated the game with colorful uniforms (for better visual appeal), night play (for higher audience ratings during prime time), and live balls, lowered mounds, and smaller strike zones (for more action) to make baseball more attractive to viewers and, thus, to advertisers. "At best, ballpark spectators have become the equivalent of studio guests," wrote historian Allen Guttmann. "At worst, they are background, mere television props."[7]

One baseball romantic summarized these critiques: "Baseball is a game that was designed to be played on a sunny afternoon in Wrigley Field in the 1920s, not on a 21-inch screen."[8] Despite the criticism, television's influence on baseball is here to stay, much to the dismay of those who would prefer to sit in old ballparks with natural grass and watch pitchers in drab flannel uniforms hit for themselves on sunny afternoons.

Observers also say that television changed the nature of media coverage of sports. "Telling readers who won and how the runs were scored no longer sufficed," said one sports editor to *Sports Illustrated* writer Rick Telander. "We had to tell readers more about the players as personalities, delve more thoroughly into the reasons for strategies, be more critical of managers and coaches, and report more thoroughly the behind-the-scenes maneuvering and conflicts."[9] Thus, the sports cliché was elevated to an art form as players learned how to face the beat writers' insatiable appetites for quotes to fill game stories.

Texas beat writer Phil Rogers offered his perspective on the matter in a personal interview at Arlington Stadium in 1989: "When there was no great influence from television, baseball was easier to cover. Some of the Damon Runyons who waxed poetic also didn't write about games that started at 7:35 P.M. to be in prime time. The nightly deadlines have taken a lot of the joy out of writing."

Finally, today's sports media cover the athlete's off-the-field problems far more than they did several years ago. "It's because of Watergate," said Tracy Ringolsby, another Texas beat writer. Most analysts locate the origin of this trend a few years before Watergate when our country witnessed the escalation of social protest, the development of Tom Wolfe's "New Journalism" as a form of reporting, and the publication of a new series of "kiss-and-tell" sports books, such as Jim Bouton's *Ball Four*, which was released in 1970. What once was considered taboo in the days of Babe Ruth is now considered "good copy" that sells newspapers and makes careers.

Rick Telander provided the perfect example of this change in sports when he told the story about a group of beat writers traveling by train with the New York Yankees in 1928. The group watched in awe as an attractive young woman wielding a knife chased after Babe Ruth yelling, "I'll kill you, you son of a bitch." One of the writers said, "That'd make a helluva story," as his colleagues laughed and continued to play poker, knowing that the story would never be written. Telander revealed that the story was finally written forty-eight years later when one of the writers was in his eighties.[10]

Is there any doubt that if the Babe were playing today, he would be a regular feature in *National Enquirer* and on television's "Hard Copy"?

Do Sports in the Media Reflect Society?

Many scholarly and popular writers have argued that sports and their coverage in the media reflect society and the changes that have taken place in society over the years. Political scientist Richard Lipsky wrote that "sport is the symbolic expression of the values of the larger political and social milieu." Sociologist Harry Edwards concurred, arguing that sport assists in "disseminating and reinforcing the values regulating behavior and goal attainment . . . and regulating perceptions of life in general."[11]

Of course, sports do not reflect American society by themselves. People produce, manage, and cover sports to mirror certain aspects of society. Thus, sports do not really reflect society as much as the beliefs and values of those in positions of power, including members of the mass media. Consequently, it is more accurate to say that sports are used by some to "reinforce" certain values and beliefs.

Early proponents of baseball, for example, wrote that those who played the game developed important virtues. Spalding's widely read *America's National Game*, published in 1911, suggested that by playing baseball, people learned "American courage, confidence, combativeness; American dash, discipline, determination; American energy, eagerness, enthusiasm; American pluck, persistence, performance; American spirit, sagacity, success; American vim, vigor, virility." William McKeever's popular advice manual *Training the Boy*, published in 1913, suggested, "No boy can grow to a perfectly normal manhood today without the benefits of at least a small amount of baseball experience and practice."[12]

American presidents over the years have extolled the virtues of baseball. Theodore Roosevelt listed baseball in his list of "the true sports for a manly race." Herbert Hoover once said that "next to religion, baseball has furnished a greater impact on American life than any other institution." Most presidents since William Taft have continued to endorse ceremonially the importance of baseball in society by throwing out the first ball to mark the opening of the season. As vice-president, George Bush even played in an old-timers' game in 1984 (going one for two: a pop-up off Warren Spahn and a single off Milt Pappas).[13]

Baseball no longer holds the exclusive patent on our national consciousness since the emergence of American football as the most watched sport on television, but writers suggest that our "national pastime" continues to reflect society. Thomas Boswell used this continued belief in the clever title of one book of essays, *How Life Imitates the World Series*.

And writers continue to cite Jacques Barzun's overused maxim that "Whoever wants to know the heart and mind of America had better learn baseball."[14]

Members of the mass media play perhaps the most powerful role in reinforcing certain aspects of society in their coverage of baseball and other sports. On some occasions, members of the sports media emphasize values and beliefs directly, as when columnists or color commentators openly endorse or criticize the playing practices or life-styles of athletes. On most occasions, however, reporters and broadcasters reinforce their value preferences subtly through descriptions of game events and player profiles. In either case, as sports critic John Hargreaves argued, media coverage of sport transforms athletes into "personifications of certain kinds of values," and the media becomes "part of the wider process whereby particular kinds of life styles, values, and ideas are 'sold.'"[15]

The average fan does not look for the values and beliefs endorsed in media stories of sports. The average fan wants to know what happened in the game and how the game outcome influenced the standings of their team or the statistics of a favorite player. But if certain societal values and beliefs are being reinforced directly or indirectly through mediated sports, it is important to examine the kinds of values and beliefs that are being perpetuated.

In this book, I look at the kinds of values and beliefs promoted in media coverage of Nolan Ryan. This book, then, is not a biography about the "real" life of Nolan Ryan on the mound or at the ranch; it is a look at the media-covered life of Nolan Ryan in print and on television. For the players who have faced Nolan Ryan, his meaning on the mound has been clear: watch out for a 95 MPH fastball thrown high and tight, just under the chin, followed by an 80 MPH curveball that could drop off the table and buckle the knees. But for those who have read about Nolan Ryan or seen him on television pitching baseballs for the Rangers or pitching pain-killers for Advil, his meaning in American culture is not so clear.

In coming chapters, I look at media coverage of Ryan throughout his career, from the struggles of his early years with the Mets to the triumphs of his final years with the Rangers. I explore how Ryan's presence affected the Rangers franchise, from the front office management to the front gate workers, and beyond into the community. I discuss media representations of Ryan as a hero of old, particularly the portrayal of Ryan's career as a narrative quest. I describe the commodification and promotion of Ryan's image by the media, his teams, and himself and look at the effect on his status as American hero. I assess the images of masculinity that society and the media associated with Ryan and subsequently reinforced. And I conclude by examining the American values at play in the media's portrayal of Nolan Ryan. As we read articles and watch programs to learn more about Nolan Ryan and his remarkable career, we also learn more about the mass media and their remarkable ability to *reinforce* certain images of American culture. I hope this book reveals as much about the American sports media as it does about the American sports hero, Nolan Ryan.

From Wild Western Prodigy to the Ageless Wonder

"Ryan . . . could be the next Sandy Koufax."
—LIFE, 1968

"Some day Ryan may strike out 27."
—THE SPORTING NEWS, 1974

"God is good. But Nolan Ryan may be better."
—DALLAS MORNING NEWS, 1990

When nineteen-year-old phenom Nolan Ryan made his major league debut with the New York Mets in September, 1966, Lyndon Baines Johnson was president, young men still were being drafted to serve in the escalating Vietnam conflict, and Jimmy Hendricks and the Doors were on the top of the popular music charts. Six presidents and countless musical trends later, forty-six-year-old Nolan Ryan continued to throw 90 MPH fastballs in 1993, his record-setting twenty-seventh season in the major leagues. I begin by chronicling how the media covered the ups and downs of Ryan's remarkable career.

Members of the sports media have faced many decisions about how to cover Ryan throughout his career. Obviously, his milestone strikeouts and no-hitters had to be covered extensively because they were newsworthy sports events, but sportswriters and sportscasters made many choices, consciously and unconsciously about how to present Ryan and his accomplishments. Not surprisingly, this media coverage changed as Ryan's career evolved from his early days as the "wild prodigy" with the New York Mets to his later years as the "ageless wonder" with the Texas Rangers.[1]

New York Mets (1966–71): The Unfulfilled Promise of a Wild Western Prodigy

In his major league debut with the Mets on September 11, 1966, Nolan Ryan pitched two full innings against the Atlanta Braves, giving up one run (earned) on one hit, striking out three, and walking one. In his next and final appearance of 1966, on September 18, Ryan's performance was more erratic, and in summarizing the outing, *New York Times* reporter Leonard Koppett foreshadowed Ryan's career as a Met: "Ryan lasted only one inning, in which he struck out the side, but he also gave up four runs on four hits, two walks and a wild pitch."[2]

The Tall Texan with "the Fastest Fastball in Town"

Early coverage of Ryan focused on the unique ability of this young rural Texan to throw the ball hard. Even in the minor leagues, Ryan attracted press coverage about his unique power. "The 20-year-old native of Alvin, Tex., hasn't started a game for the Jacksonville Sons," wrote one reporter of Ryan's minor league stint in Florida in 1967, "but his fastball is the talk of the league." In the same article, however, the reporter offered this misguided observation: "There's one big difference between Ryan and most young fastballers. He isn't wild." The *New York Times* story of his debut against the Braves noted his minor league record of 422 strikeouts in 369 innings and added that "no one succeeded in getting around on Ryan."[3]

Reporters called Ryan "the rookie pitcher with the cannonball serve" and the "Texas flame-thrower." A *Life* magazine feature revealed that he had "a fast ball that has been described as faster than Bob Feller's (98.6 MPH) — the fastest ever timed."[4] In these and other articles, the media presented the young Ryan's on-the-field persona to the public as a power pitcher.

Suffering "Early Inning Blues": Adversity on and off the Field

At the same time, reporters also wrote that Ryan would have to overcome adversity before realizing his rare talent. Sportswriters often reminded readers that he could not throw the ball where he wanted to throw it. He was the "tall, slim Texan . . . who has not yet mastered control and consistency"; more metaphorically, he was "as wild as the spinning Black Dragon ride at Astroworld."[5] In fact, Ryan admitted his control problems, saying that "the wildness has been a problem right from the start, right from when I was 5 years old and couldn't throw the ball to my brother who was standing 5 yards away."[6] Years later the press still reminded readers of Ryan's wild early days. "He was wild as a March hare," remembered his high school coach in one story. "He had a hard time hitting the mitt."[7]

Reporters also criticized Ryan because he was unable to play on a full-time basis with the Mets. After a rare start and complete game victory in 1970, Joe Durso of the *New York Times* called him "the most spectacular part-time employee in baseball," explaining that Ryan had not pitched more often because of "blisters on his fingers," "Army reserve duty," and "his father's illness and death." Durso concluded that "as a result of all the problems, Ryan has never pitched a full season in six years of professional baseball."[8]

Ryan's wildness and his status as a "part-time" player kept him from emerging as a regular pitcher for the Mets – and from establishing a media identity as a key contributor to the team. During the 1969 championship season of the "Miracle Mets," Ryan was conspicuously absent from the pitching mound. He pitched only 89.0 total innings that season, the third lowest in his career (he pitched 66.1 innings in his 1993 final season). In the 1969 World Series, he pitched just 2.1 innings as a reliever in Game 3, though he was credited with the save.

During this time Ryan was absent from media coverage as well. Ryan's name was not even mentioned in an article by Leonard Koppett titled "The 'Yout' of America," a surprising omission because part of the team's success was credited to the "good young pitching," including that of Ryan's more successful teammates "Terrific" Tom Seaver, Jerry Koosman, and Gary Gentry.

Neither Prospect nor Suspect

As the media contrasted Ryan's raw ability to throw hard with his inability to overcome his wildness, they set the stage for his baseball odyssey and for the ultimate celebration of him as sports hero and celebrity. If Ryan could not control his unique ability, he and his "heat" would be just a flash in the pan, and he would fail as many fastball pitchers had failed before him. But if Ryan could overcome this obstacle and master his skill, as *Life* magazine put it, he "could be the next Sandy Koufax."

After three up-and-down seasons with the Mets, reporters wondered if Ryan ever would pan out. One headline during spring training in 1971 asked the question, "Ryan – Trade Him or Wait"? The reporter suggested that "the only reason [Ryan] may still be with the team is because the Mets can't get what they want for him in a deal."[9]

Ryan would not fulfill his potential with the Mets. His last appearance in a Met uniform came on September 28, 1971, against the Cardinals, when he started the game and failed to get an out. The newspaper reported the grim details: "Ryan walked the first four men he faced, forcing in one run, and then gave up a two-run single to Ted Simmons, the Cardinal catcher." The story noted that "yesterday's defeat was the 15th consecutive incomplete start for Ryan, who now has a 10-14 won-lost record."[10]

On December 10, 1971, Ryan and three others were traded to the California Angels for infielder Jim Fregosi and three others. "The New York Mets finally gave up on Nolan Ryan's wandering fastball yesterday," wrote Durso in the *New York Times*, adding that Met General Manager Bob Scheffing had said: "I really can't say I quit on him. But we've had him three full years and although he's a hell of a prospect, he hasn't done it for us. How long can you wait?"[11]

A Los Angeles sportswriter quoted Angel general manager Harry Dalton, who said this about Ryan's promise: "We've obtained the best arm in the National League and one of the best in baseball. We know Ryan has had control problems, but at 24 he may be ready to come into his own."[12] At this point, the media showed Ryan as "the best arm" in baseball, who might develop into a complete pitcher.

Ryan expressed dissatisfaction with his image as "prospect" before the 1972 season in a feature article by Ross Newhan. "I hate to hear people still refer to me as a prospect because after four years in the majors I should have achieved more than I have," Ryan said. "I'm not a prospect but neither should I be suspect." Ryan admitted that his "own lack of maturity and self control" had hampered his success, but he accused Mets management of failing to help him with his problems, saying "I never achieved anything with the Mets because I never received any instruction." In the same article, Newhan used Ryan's own words to characterize the significance of the first phase of his career, a phase that prophesied his potential: "I guess the suffering now will make success that much more enjoyable—if it comes."[13]

California Angels (1972–79): A Second Chance at Stardom

Ryan welcomed his trade to the Angels, as did the team and the ever-present sports media. Ryan characterized his Mets years as a constant trial that had ended, and he described himself as "a rookie making a fresh start."

Angel at Crossroads

"No more talk of promise," declared one writer on the day of Ryan's American League debut. "No more compaprisons with Sandy Koufax in velocity of fastball or in how Ryan, like Koufax, has had to struggle with control." In the article Ryan said, "I'm simply at the point of my career where I have to prove myself," adding, "I have to get the ball over the plate or I'll find myself in the same situation I was in frequently with the Mets."[14]

Ryan's second chance started with familiar press coverage. His identity as a power pitcher again was embellished—as was his status as incomplete prospect. After a 6-3 loss to the Oakland A's early in the season, one story used power-hitter Reggie Jackson's cliché-ridden description of Ryan's pitching prowess: "He's faster than instant coffee. He's faster than a speeding bullet and more powerful than a locomotive. He throws wall-to-wall heat." In the article Jackson concluded that, although Ryan was still only a prospect, "when he finally becomes a complete pitcher . . . there will be no way to hit him."[15]

Ryan's second chance started with familiar pitching stats as well. He won his debut with the Angels, pitching a 2-0 shutout over the Minnesota Twins, but then lost his next two starts. After he lasted just two innings in a 12-2 loss against the Orioles in late April, one reporter reviewed the Ryan-Fregosi trade and concluded that "early returns are running against [Angel GM Harry] Dalton." The same reporter added that "there are whispers that Ryan's wildness stems from his unwillingness to take instruction." He also revealed that Angel manager Del Rice was so disappointed by the loss that he had admitted: "We'll decide within the next few days if Nolan will stay in the rotation. We can't keep him there if he's going to walk 5 or 6 every time."[16]

The Leap to Stardom
Ryan stayed in the rotation and improved dramatically in his first season with the Angels. He ended the year with a 19-16 record and set several Angel strikeout records. Then, in the next few years, Ryan began to overcome his erraticness and become a star on the playing field. In 1973 and 1974 he achieved the traditional measure of pitching success: 20 games won (21-16 and 22-16, respectively). In 1973 he became the fourth pitcher in history to throw two no-hitters; at the end of that year, he set a record of 383 strikeouts in one season with his "high voltage fast ball," breaking Sandy Koufax's record of 382.

In 1974 Ryan threw his third no-hitter, and Rockwell scientists clocked his pitches during a game at speeds of 100.8 and 100.9 MPH, the fastest pitches ever recorded. In 1975 he threw another no-hitter, to become "a hitless wonder for the fourth time," tying Koufax's all-time record. Through these historical and highly publicized pitching performances, Ryan fulfilled those earlier promises of greatness and was granted a lasting place in baseball lore by sportswriters. In Boston sports columnist Melvin Durslag called Ryan "the most exciting of all pitchers." Dick Miller outrageously suggested that "some day Ryan may strike out 27." Ron Fimrite described Ryan thus: "A man who can throw as hard as Nolan Ryan is no ordinary mortal. He is among the blessed, an exalted figure to be held in awe."[17]

At this point, reporters began reinterpreting the trade of Fregosi for Ryan as one of the most one-sided trades in baseball. Writing for the *New York Times*, Dave Anderson called it "a trade that will live in infamy." In the *New York Post*, Larry Merchant compared it with "the Dodgers failing to protect Roberto Clemente in the minor league draft" and "the Cubs giving up on the young Lou Brock."[18]

Ryan also became a star in the popular press, acquiring more publicity with each milestone. In 1974 he won a Los Angeles Press Club award as a headline-maker. In 1975 his picture was displayed in an advertisement for cowboy boots in *Playboy* magazine; he also made a cameo appearance on the soap opera *Ryan's Hope*. Thanks to his presence on the mound and in the media, he had become, as *Newsweek* labeled him, a "superstar." *Sport* magazine inaccurately predicted that Nolan Ryan would not remain a celebrity for long because "he's not the type for the gossip columns" and "he's too homespun, too quiet, too private." But Ryan's traditional values and his understated life-style actually contributed to his media identity as hero and celebrity.[19]

Still Mortal after All These Feats

Although the media celebrated Ryan's unprecedented success as a superstar Angel, they also described his continued struggles as a mere mortal. Sportswriters revealed that Ryan experienced major back and arm problems during the 1975 season that limited the number of innings he pitched (from a league-leading 333.0 in 1974 to 198.0) and cut his won-lost record (from 22-16 in 1974 to 14-12). Yet, whereas the New York media had cast his injuries as obstacles to his (and the Mets') success, his injuries as an Angel—and his choice to play despite these injuries—were now cast by the media in heroic terms. "The 14 games he won in 1975 and the 4th career no-hitter he pitched may one day be looked upon as his greatest feats," wrote Ron Rapoport in the *Los Angeles Times*, because "from his 4th start of the season, his arm was all but falling off."[20]

Ryan's critics, however, charged that he was not only mortal, but also mediocre, at least in the won-lost column. Despite his legendary feats as an Angel, Ryan's career record after the 1979 season was 167-159, and he had been just 138-121 as an Angel. Although Ryan had been hampered by injuries during the time he pitched his fourth no-hitter and his teams had provided little support for him, Ryan's won-lost record was the subject of sustained criticism.

One of Ryan's toughest critics, according to the sports media, was new Angel general manager Buzzie Bavasi. When Ryan and Bavasi failed to agree on a new contract for the 1980 season, Ryan became an unrestricted free agent, and Bavasi told reporters that he could replace Ryan "with two 8-7 pitchers," a sarcastic reference to Ryan's 16-14 record in 1979. Ryan himself wrote a letter "to the fans of the California Angels," which was published in the *Orange County Register* sports section on November 15, 1979. After thanking the fans and saying that he would "never forget you and your cheers and your loyalty," he ended with a veiled jab at Bavasi: "To the extent I feel there were certain officials who made it nearly impossible for me to stay, I would hope that they have learned from the experience and will not repeat their mistakes with others." Years later, an Angel vice-president who had been the club's director of public relations when Ryan was not re-signed admitted that the Angel fans "were ready to crucify Buzzie" because "Nolan was adored here."[21]

Although Bavasi did not make a serious attempt to re-sign Ryan, reporters wrote that at least thirteen teams were pursuing this "star of today's re-entry draft of free agents." *Sports Illustrated* quoted then–Yankee owner George Steinbrenner as saying that Ryan was "one of the most desirable quantities in baseball," a telling comment that indicated both Ryan's attractiveness as a star pitcher and his marketability as a superstar celebrity.[22] Ryan exercised his free agency and signed a contract with the Houston Astros on November 19, 1979.

Houston Astros (1980–88):
Coming Home to Millions,
More Milestones, and More Mediocrity

Nolan Ryan signed a free agent contract worth a record $1 million per year for three years with the Astros, who had an option on a fourth year for $1 million. *Sport* magazine reported that the contract made Ryan the "best-paid player in the history of baseball." Another report quibbled that it made him only "the game's highest-paid free agent signee," noting that the Pirates' Dave Parker also was a million-dollar-a-year player.[23]

Ryan's contract drew mixed reviews in the sports pages. *Sport* magazine described it as a "$4 million gamble" because of his history of injuries. Even so, the article reminded readers that there were two powerful reasons why Ryan probably was worth the money: because of the "money-in-the-bank drama in every start," which could draw fans in anticipation of another no-hitter, and because "Nolan Ryan is 'home country'" who "won't simply draw fans to the ballpark; he'll draw friends."[24]

The Celebrated Homecoming

After his mass media odyssey from one end of the country to the other, the "eternal country boy" returned home to Texas, close to the town of Alvin, where he was raised and where he still lives and raises cattle. "Baseball has taken Nolan Ryan to both coasts, but it has never taken him out of Alvin," wrote Ron Fimrite in *Sports Illustrated*. "It's what he's all about."[25]

Through the media, readers returned home vicariously with Nolan. Readers went to Nolan's childhood home on Dezso Drive, the house just past the "Smile, Jesus Loves You" sign where his mom still lived. They traveled up Gordon Street, where Nolan "used to roll 1,500 newspapers a night" to help his dad earn extra money from a paper route. They met Nolan's close friends, including one who said that Nolan "always had it in his mind to pitch in Texas" and that "everybody in Alvin is real excited about it."[26]

The media celebration of Ryan's return as hometown hero reaffirmed his new Astros' identity as a "regular guy," despite his astronomical salary. Ryan's barber Larry, who had cut his hair for ten years, was the perfect character witness, saying that "Nolan is a super-fine fella" who "hasn't gotten a swelled head like some of those athletes with the big money." The portrait of Ryan painted by the mass media was that of "a modest and clean-living young man from rural America who has pitched uncomplainingly for generally mediocre teams."[27]

More Heat and More Milestones

Then into his late thirties, Ryan was still throwing his trademark fastball. Indeed, Ryan's still being able to throw heat was presented as a mystery, and sportswriters sought answers from various baseball sleuths. "This fantastic ability to still 'bring it' after all these years absolutely baffles the baseball savants," wrote Ron Fimrite in *Sports Illustrated*. And Fimrite quoted Ryan, who said it was "a matter of mechanics," and Dodger pitching coach Ron Perranowski, who invoked a divine explanation, saying, "God gave him one hell of an arm."[28]

In *Gentlemen's Quarterly*, Richard Hoffer quoted Yankee pitcher Tommy John, who attributed Ryan's success to the "ratio of fast-twitch nerve fibers in that arm," and former Dodger pitcher Don Sutton, who simply said that Ryan was "a freak." But Hoffer concluded that there was no adequate explanation for Ryan's continued ability: "The man has a forty-one-year-old arm that's livelier than any rookie's. No theory accounts for it, or even predicts its eventual end."[29]

Ryan continued to reach new milestones in his years with the Houston Astros, two of which were special in light of earlier prophecies. In 1981 Ryan threw his fifth no-hitter, against the Dodgers, surpassing the all-time no-hit record he and Sandy Koufax had shared since 1974. "It's hard to believe I got the no-hitter," Ryan was quoted as saying after the game. "It's the one thing I wanted. I've had a shot at it for a long time. At my age, I thought I wouldn't get it."[30]

In 1983 he recorded his 3,509th strikeout, against Brad Mills of Montreal, and the "Ryan Express" surpassed "Big Train" Walter Johnson as baseball's all-time strikeout leader, breaking a record that had stood for fifty-six years. Years later Mills recalled: "I was looking for a fastball [but] he threw me a curveball and I got vapor-locked."[31]

In 1985 Ryan recorded an unprecedented 4,000th strikeout. Pete Axthelm described this historic achievement in this way: "He had painted the Picasso and defined greatness on his own terms. . . . He had blended the 100-mile-an-hour flashes of brilliance with a leathery ranch hand's longevity. In the words of yet another Southern perfectionist named William Faulkner, he had not only endured but prevailed. It was time to quiet all questions about whether Nolan Ryan was a winner."[32]

Still Mediocre after All These Years

Despite Ryan's achievements, questions about his status as a winner remained. Critics grumbled about his mediocre record when he first signed with the Astros for multi-millions. "He's won numerous battles," wrote one sports reporter, "but he keeps losing the war." The same reporter also quoted Ryan's own reluctant, and somewhat defiant, admission: "Maybe I've lost too many games to be considered a great pitcher. But it's always bothered other people more than it's bothered me."[33]

Questions were also raised after his first season with the Astros when he posted an 11-10 record in return for his $1 million salary. And after nine seasons in Houston, his career record as an Astro was just 106-94 while his entire major league career record was just 273-253. One report indicated that "compared with the records of the best pitchers of his generation, Ryan's win numbers come up woefully short"; another over-simplified Ryan's career in bottom-line terms: "He is not a winner."[34]

Some critics wrote that his continued, if somewhat controlled, wild-ness led to many of his defeats; one report quoted Ryan's admission that "I definitely beat myself sometimes with walks." Another quoted Tom Morgan, his pitching coach on the Angels, as saying: "Nolie thought he had to pitch to spots. . . . I felt if he would throw for the middle of the plate, he would've been better, but he said he didn't feel he could pitch that way." Others charged that Ryan was overly aggressive, that he was "too macho on the mound" because he "wanted to challenge every hitter" and "strike him out."[35]

Ryan's defenders countered that he had played for weak teams through-out his career. One article in 1983 showed that Ryan had a career record of twenty games over .500, while his teams had a combined record of four-teen games *under* .500 without him. Former Dodger pitcher Don Sutton was a witness for the defense, quoted as saying that Ryan has "been in the wrong place at the wrong time with the right stuff."[36]

After nine seasons with Houston, Ryan again found himself without a team as Astro management refused to sign him at the end of the 1988 season. He became a free agent for the second time on November 1, 1988, and it looked as though the hometown hero would pack up again and move back to the West Coast.

Texas Rangers (1989–93): Vindication at Last for the Ageless Wonder

Nolan Ryan was signed as a free agent by the Texas Rangers on December 7, 1988, at the baseball winter meetings in Atlanta, an act then–Ranger manager Bobby Valentine described as "the one most im-portant transaction the Texas Rangers have ever made." Ryan signed for a reported $1.6 million salary for the 1989 season, with a signing bonus and incentives that put the contract worth close to $2 million; the Rang-ers also had an option for the 1990 season worth $1.4 million.

When Ryan signed with the Rangers, General Manager Tom Grieve, sensitive about Ryan's status as a celebrity drawing card, told reporters that "we are not doing this for image; we are doing this because Nolan Ryan is a pitcher who can win baseball games." Despite Grieve's assertion, Dallas sportswriters claimed that Ryan gave the Rangers "new credibility," that his signing was "one incredible PR coup," and that in obtaining Ryan, the Rangers purchased "an image."[37]

In Houston and nearby Alvin, however, the news was not well-received. The Houston media cast December 7 as another "date which will live in infamy." One report quoted an anonymous Ryan fan who said, "Years from now, when school children are asked what disastrous event happened on Dec. 7, they'll say: 'That's the day Nolan Ryan went to Dallas.'"[38]

A Superstar of Epic Proportions
As a Ranger, Ryan solidifed his status as superstar as he set more records on the mound and received more publicity in the media. Media coverage of his Ranger milestones, including his 5,000th strikeout, his sixth and seventh no-hitters, and his 300th victory, reached new heights. For example, as he approached and then registered his 5,000th strikeout, the media covered the event as a truly historic occasion. For observers not interested in baseball, the game was the epitome of what Daniel Boorstin would have called a "pseudo-event," since Ryan already led the major leagues in career strikeouts, and every additional strikeout was a new milestone. But sportswriters interpreted and presented the landmark figure of 5,000 strikeouts with unprecedented fervor. Stories about the strikeout filled the major dailies across the country, and special multi-page sections on Ryan filled local papers. The August 28, 1989, issue of *Sports Illustrated* even printed the complete list of Ryan's 1,061 separate strikeout victims.

When he achieved his seventh no-hitter in 1991, sportswriters again issued glowing praise for Ryan. Steve Wulf wrote, "So now Nolan Ryan has as many no-hitters as there are seas, heavens, wonders of the world, days of the week, sacraments, deadly sins, and innings before you stretch."[39]

Ryan's identity as celebrity reached new heights with the Rangers as well when he (and the Ranger franchise) received unprecedented local publicity in a city usually dominated by the Dallas Cowboys. The media heaped more national publicity on Ryan as he became the second Ranger player ever to appear on the cover of *Sports Illustrated*—and he appeared on the cover *twice*.[40] His status as a commercial spokesman also soared, as he promoted national products including Advil, Bic shavers, BizMart office supplies, Duracell batteries, Nike, Whataburger, and Wrangler Jeans, to name a few. Ryan's commercial endorsements even became the focus of a front page story in the *Dallas Morning News*.[41]

Vindication at Last
At the time of his 5,000th strikeout, a few critics still challenged Ryan's success as a pitcher. In the papers, Hall of Fame pitcher Bob Feller offered

the most stinging critique. Dallas columnist Frank Luksa wrote that Feller had discredited Ryan's strikeout record by asserting that "strikeouts are easier to get now [because] . . . players don't care about striking out." The same columnist also said that Feller did not believe Ryan should be inducted into the Hall of Fame because he had not won 100 more games than he had lost.[42]

Surprisingly, Tracy Ringolsby quoted the normally humble and low-key Ryan as responding, "It doesn't bother me. I know where Bob Feller is coming from. He has an ego that won't fit in a ballpark, and people don't talk and write about him anymore, so he has to talk about himself."[43]

Then, on July 31, 1990, at age forty-three, Nolan Ryan won his 300th game, becoming only the twentieth pitcher in the history of baseball to do so. It was another milestone—one that symbolized success and achievement in terms of bottom-line victories. The Associated Press story on Ryan's victory over the Milwaukee Brewers began with this lead: "Nolan Ryan, a pitcher defined by great numbers, finally got the number that defines great pitchers."[44]

Sportswriters celebrated the milestone victory with unabated hyperbole. Writing for *The Sporting News*, Joe Gergen called Ryan an "icon in the heart of Texas," and he wrote, "Always at home on the range, Ryan was destined to make history on the mound."[45] Dallas sportswriter Randy Galloway spelled out what the victory meant, writing that, "300 is a number that signifies present and future generations that here stands a W-I-N-N-E-R." He then deified Ryan: "God is good. But Nolan Ryan may be better."[46]

In attaining his 300th career victory, Ryan vindicated himself from long-time critics, including Bob Feller, who reportedly retracted his earlier statement and admitted that Ryan now deserved to be in the Hall of Fame, though he still insisted that Ryan "has been pretty inconsistent in his career."[47]

Dallas sportswriter Barry Horn, commenting on Ryan's critics, wrote that "No. 300 cuts their vocal chords," while David Casstevens wrote that the 300 mark "represents a triumphant and unarguable validation of the man and his heroic career."[48] In these and other published stories, Ryan's three hundredth victory provided vindication for the Texas Ranger pitcher, as well as for the many members of the sports media who had invested so much time and so many pages covering and celebrating Nolan Ryan's career.

Farewell, Finally
On Thursday, February 11, 1993, Nolan Ryan made the announcement that some fans imagined might never come: Ryan would retire after the 1993 season. In the days following his announcement, tributes from sportswriters filled newspapers across the country. "When Ryan is gone, there's

not another one waiting in the baseball wings. Not now, maybe not ever," wrote Randy Galloway for the *Dallas Morning News*. Gordon Edes of the Fort Lauderdale *Sun-Sentinel* offered a similar tribute, writing that "when it comes to larger-than-life characters, those in the [Michael] Jordanesque category, baseball's list begins and ends with Ryan."[49]

Other sportswriters eulogized Ryan. "What he gave the Rangers," wrote Ringolsby in the *Rocky Mountain News*, "was an official state hero . . . which puts him in a class with such historical dignitaries as Davy Crockett and Sam Houston." Writing for *The Sporting News*, Dave Kindred waxed poetic about Ryan:

> Yaz is gone Rose is gone
> Aaron McCovey Banks Bench Schmidt
> the Beatles Elvis hot pants mood rings pet rocks
> 7 presidents 5 commissioners XXVII Super Bowls
> Kareem Magic Bird Payton come and gone
> while you, Nolan, brought the heat.[50]

And sportswriters continued to pay their respects to Ryan throughout the 1993 season as he conducted his farewell tour.

Nolan Ryan's Career as a Media Quest

As Ryan's career has unfolded, moments from his early years have been reinterpreted by sportswriters revising baseball history to correspond to his ultimate success. His trade from the Mets to the Angels in 1971 received little criticism from writers at the time, but the trade was seen later as "one-sided" and as one that would "live in infamy." Ryan's nagging injuries during his years with the Mets were presented by sportswriters then as problems that prevented him from pitching well, but in later years, his ability to pitch with injuries—whether he won or lost—was praised as heroic.

Some of Ryan's later non-record-breaking milestones were presented as more historic than his record-breaking accomplishments in earlier years. For example, Ryan's 3,509th strikeout, which broke Walter Johnson's all-time strikeout record, received relatively limited press coverage. In fact, Hal Bodley noted in a very brief *USA Today* story that Ryan's record-breaking strikeout was "ignored by baseball brass."[51] Yet his 4,000th and especially his 5,000th strikeouts, which merely added to his record, were cast in more historic terms and attracted more notice.

Examined historically, Ryan's career as presented by the media can be read as a narrative *quest*. As described by literary critic Northrop Frye, the narrative of the quest evolves as the character experiences *agon*, conflict and preliminary adventures; *pathos*, the crucial struggle with a neme-

sis; and *anagnorisis*, the discovery and recognition of the character as a
genuine hero.[52]

Ryan's media-narrated journey began in pastoral Little League baseball
in rural Texas and moved to Major League Baseball in New York City
and Los Angeles as he sought the American Dream of success. During
his odyssey, Ryan struggled to overcome obstacles, including wildness, injuries, and the mediocrity of his teams. These obstacles were used by his
critics, his nemeses, to challenge and threaten his quest. Along the way
he performed great feats, setting strikeout records and racking up no-hitters,
but his critics continued to challenge him. In the end, he achieved his
300th victory, overcoming his sportswriting nemeses, and became exalted
as a genuine hero worthy of baseball's most precious and lasting gift: a
place in the Hall of Fame.

Perhaps most important, Ryan returned home a hero, bringing symbolic closure to the narrative of his quest. As the late A. Bartlett Giamatti
wrote: "If baseball is Narrative, it is . . . the story . . . of going home after
having left home, the story of how difficult it is to find the origins one
so deeply needs to find. It is the literary mode called Romance."[53]

It must be remembered that this quest is an invention of the media;
Ryan did not set out to enact his life as an epic story. As he admitted
during a press conference on the day before his first, but unsuccessful,
attempt to win his 300th game in July, 1990: "My goal when I first made
the big leagues was to play for four years so I could qualify for the pension, because it took four years in the big leagues to qualify for the pension. That was a goal of mine. And there were many times with the Mets
when I thought that was in doubt."

Members of the media also have emphasized the historic nature of
Ryan's strikeouts, no-hitters, and career victories, even though Ryan himself did not see them as historic accomplishments at the time. As he said
during the same press conference, "I don't think winning 300 changes my
won-lost record, so I don't view 300 in any special way as far as quieting
critics. I think that I get a lot of satisfaction out of the fact that I've been
able to pitch as long as I have and maintain the style of pitcher I've been
throughout my career."

Indeed, when asked at the press conference following his 5,000th strikeout in August, 1989, "Where do you see your place in baseball history?"
Ryan responded: "I don't know. You know, to be honest, I don't think
about those things. My attitude is, I just concern myself with what's going on in getting ready for my next start. In the morning, I'll get up and
be back over here in the weight room getting ready for the Angels on
Sunday."

1. The young Nolan Ryan as a New York Met. Courtesy National Baseball
Library, Cooperstown, N.Y.

2. Ryan breaks Sandy Koufax's single-season strikeout record in 1973 against the Minnesota Twins. Courtesy National Baseball Library, Cooperstown, N.Y.

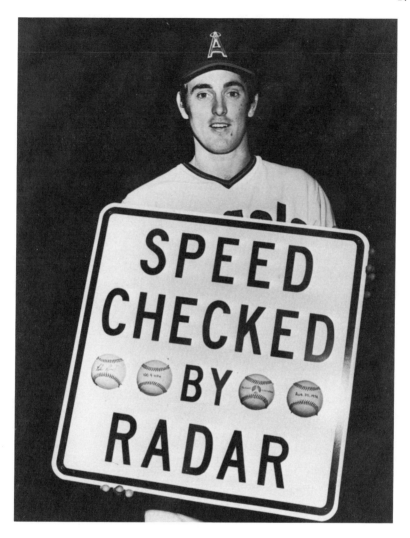

3. In 1974 Rockwell scientists clocked a Ryan pitch at 100.9 MPH, the fastest pitch ever thrown. Courtesy National Baseball Library, Cooperstown, N.Y.

4. Ryan warms up in bullpen before his fourth no-hitter, a game against the Baltimore Orioles in 1975. Photo by Harry Holstine.

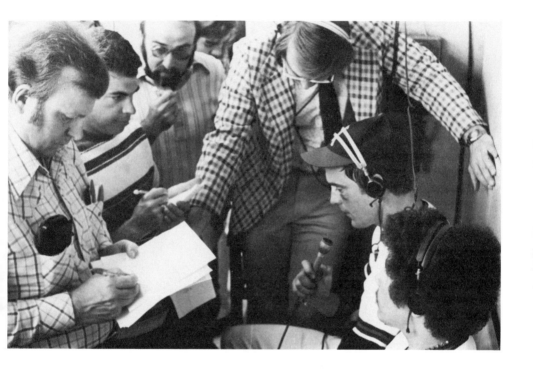

5. Ryan talks about his fourth no-hitter with the ever-present media. Photo by Harry Holstine.

6. Ryan walks off the field after getting his 5,000th strikeout, pitching against the Oakland Athletics in 1989. Photo by Linda Kaye.

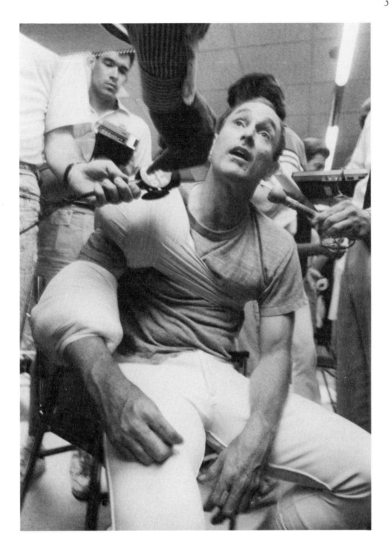

7. Ryan talks to reporters in locker room after his seventh no-hitter, in 1991.
Photo by Linda Kaye.

8. To develop proper throwing mechanics, Ryan uses a technique of former Ranger pitching coach Tom House. Photo by Brad Newton.

9. Ryan signs historic contract with Rangers in 1991. Pictured clockwise are Ryan, managing partner George W. Bush, president Thomas Schieffer, general manager Tom Grieve, and general partner Edward (Rusty) Rose. Photo by Linda Kaye.

10. Ryan announces that the 1993 season, his record-breaking twenty-seventh in the major leagues, will be his final one. Photo by Linda Kaye.

Nolan Ryan's Meaning to the Texas Rangers

"You wouldn't believe the number of calls we get from people when we're on the road who say, 'I named my son after Nolan Ryan and I'd like to meet him when you come to Cleveland.'"
VICE-PRESIDENT, PUBLIC RELATIONS

"I remember when I was working here as a gate supervisor in my late teens. It was a Sunday afternoon and I just left my gate about the third inning because I was going to see Nolan Ryan pitch from behind home plate. I stood there for about four innings with my gate completely unattended. Of course, if one of my people did that now, I'd go through the roof."
DIRECTOR, STADIUM OPERATIONS

"There was no way I wasn't gonna work out here this year with Nolan Ryan pitching. He's awesome."
TEENAGE PARKING LOT ATTENDANT

Baseball fans appreciate Nolan Ryan because of his impressive accomplishments and lengthy career in the major leagues. But Nolan Ryan has special meaning to those who have played or worked for his teams. In this chapter, I look specifically at Ryan's significance to members of the Texas Ranger franchise and of the Texas media. This chapter is based on a study of franchise executives and stadium workers I conducted from October, 1987, to July, 1990. [1] When Ryan was signed by the Rangers in December, 1988, I had interviewed and observed hundreds of franchise members, from front office executives and middle managers to part-time ushers, vendors, and parking lot attendants. I learned quickly that Ryan's presence would affect the franchise in dramatic and lasting ways. So, as I continued my study during Ryan's first season in 1989, I noticed how he influenced the lives of many people associated with the Ranger franchise.

Nolan Ryan Becomes a Texas Ranger

Nolan Ryan was signed as a free agent by the Rangers on December 7, 1988, at the winter meetings in Atlanta. His signing complemented earlier trades at those meetings that brought Raphael Palmeiro (from the Chicago Cubs), Julio Franco (from the Cleveland Indians), and others. But the acquisition of Ryan was special. As Ranger manager Bobby

Valentine prophesied on that day, "Signing Nolan Ryan is the c   most important transaction the Texas Rangers ever made."

"I remember the first time I heard that Nolan was about to declare free agency after his contractual difficulties in Houston," reminisced former Ranger president Mike Stone in an interview in January, 1990. "I remember Bobby Valentine and Tom Grieve were sitting in Tom's office, and I said, 'Hey, would we have any interest in Nolan Ryan?' They both stared at me and said, 'Of course.'" But, Stone continued, "We were concerned that we wouldn't have much of a chance to sign him, and, being in Texas, we didn't want to offend Houston. So when we called Dick Moss, Nolan's agent, we told him that until Nolan made the decision not to return to Houston, we weren't really going to be serious at the table, but if he said goodbye to Houston, we would be there with everything we could bring. We knew we couldn't get into a bidding war, but we went to the Atlanta meetings knowing that we had an outside chance to sign Nolan Ryan."

Stone smiled and then told a story about those winter meetings:

When we were at the winter meetings, Nolan called and said that he and his agent were coming to Atlanta. He said he didn't want to drag the thing out or appear like he was trying to work the marketplace, which is typical Nolan. He had said goodbye to Houston, and he said he was not going to leave Atlanta unsigned.

When Nolan showed up in Atlanta, Bobby, Tommy, and I met with him that night. We were the first of three teams that were going to meet with him. [The other two teams were the California Angels and the San Francisco Giants.] And we made our pitch. We told him that we didn't consider signing him to be some freakish marketing maneuver but that we thought he could help us on the mound with his pitching and in the clubhouse with his leadership ability.

I must admit that when the three of us walked back from his hotel to the hotel where we were staying, we were not optimistic. We kept hearing rumors about what California and San Francisco were doing. We knew that [Angel owner] Gene Autry could open his rather deep pockets.

I got up about 7:00 o'clock the next morning. I had just stepped in the shower when my wife knocked on the door and said that Dick Moss was on the phone. I went to the phone shivering and he told me, "Nolan would like to meet with you right now. Can you come over to the hotel?" I said, "Sure." I got hastily dressed, didn't even shave, and called Tom's room and Bobby's room, but they were out joggin. So, I asked my wife if she could leave a message for the two of them to join me at Nolan's suite.

When I made it over there, Dick Moss greets me at the door and says, "Nolan has made up his mind. He would like to be a Texas Ranger." I couldn't believe my ears.

Ryan's signing was announced at 12:30 P.M. in Atlanta, and the reaction in Texas was immediate: the phone lines were jammed with callers inquiring about—and buying—season tickets. "I don't know the exact number," John Schriever, the director of ticket operations, recalled, "but the day we signed Nolan, the phone traffic more than tripled. We sold a lot of season tickets that day and over one hundred season tickets within a week after signing him."

Chuck Morgan, the director of broadcasting, who also serves as the Rangers' in-house announcer, also noted Ryan's immediate economic impact, not just in ticket or advertising sales, but in terms of the entire community. "The day we signed him," he remembered, "I was in the car going to speak somewhere, and on the radio the lead story was, 'In just a moment, we'll talk about the economic impact that Nolan Ryan will have on the city of Arlington.' I thought to myself, here's *one* baseball player that is going to have an effect on the entire city's economy."

Franchise members knew immediately that Ryan would be an important member of the franchise, but few predicted that Ryan would be successful on the field during his first season with the Rangers in 1989. "I knew that he would bring some credibility and some more people to the ballpark, but I was a little skeptical because he hadn't had that good a year in 1988," admitted Mat Stolley, the director of stadium operations.

As John McMichael, the vice-president of business operations put it: "In retrospect, it looks like an automatic great deal that the Rangers should have done and that we're so fortunate that Nolan said 'yes' to us. But it was not without risk. Nolan had come off a couple flat seasons. So, lost in all of this is the guts that the Rangers showed to get a guy who would be a future Hall of Famer, but who might not help the club to the tune of $1.6 million." (In retrospect, $1.6 million does not look like much of a risk with salaries hitting the $5, $6, and even $7 million per year mark in the early 1990s.)

At the time of his signing, even fewer could predict how important Ryan would become to the Ranger franchise. "Signing Ryan was a big deal," admitted John Blake, vice-president of public relations, "but the winter meetings that year were so busy that he was part of a group of players we signed including Franco and Palmeiro. I knew that he had struck out a lot of guys, but I didn't really know him that well because he had been in the National League the previous eight years. It didn't hit me about what we were getting in Nolan until I went back to Arlington and started doing research on him for the media guide. And then the requests for interviews and autographs started coming in."

During spring training in 1989, Ryan was irritated by minor leg problems and did not pitch as many innings as expected. Ryan then struggled in his first game as a Ranger, but even so, Ranger fans and workers were amazed that he was there, in Arlington Stadium, pitching for the Texas Rangers.

The Ranger Debut

Nolan Ryan made his debut as a Texas Ranger on April 6, 1989, at Arlington Stadium against the Detroit Tigers in the Rangers' second game of the 1989 season. The game had an unusual 5:00 P.M. (sharp) starting time instead of the typical 7:35 P.M. (or so) time in order to comply with a league rule that states games must begin no later than 5:00 P.M. on travel days when the next game for the traveling team is a day game (or something to that effect). Since Detroit would play its 1989 home opener the following day at 12:35 P.M., against Milwaukee, Arlington Stadium's rarely seen five o'clock shadow covered the awaiting Tigers at home plate as Nolan Ryan took to the mound in a Ranger uniform.

Ryan struck out Kenny Williams, the first Tiger hitter, much to the delight of the not-quite 25,735 fans who left work a little earlier that day to see Ryan's debut. Immediately, single K's—the letter that symbolizes a strikeout for those who keep score—were hung in at least four areas of the ballpark. A second K immediately followed as Ryan fanned Torey Lovullo. Lou Whitaker disappointed the home crowd with a single, but then Ryan struck out Alan Trammell to end the inning. And so it came to pass that Texas native Nolan Ryan struck out the side in his debut as a Texas Ranger, as if to fulfill baseball prophecy.

In attendance at Ryan's debut were about four hundred folks, or "folk," who arrived in several chartered buses from Ryan's hometown of Alvin, Texas. The caravan was led by Sheriff Joe King of Brazoria County and Alvin Mayor Allen Gray, who had coached Nolan's older brother Robert in Little League. Gray even threw out the ceremonial first pitch. The Alvin folk wore "Ryan Express" buttons and took up an entire section in the 300-level seats on the home (first base) side. Banners reading "Ryan Express: Alvin to Arlington" marked the area, and cowboy hats—*many* cowboy hats—dotted the crowd.

I purchased a seat for this historic game in the front row behind home plate—directly behind one of the backstop screen posts. It was a single seat sandwiched between groups of season ticket holders with a partially obstructed, but very close, view of Ryan on the mound. I sat next to a woman of German descent wearing a New York Rangers hockey jacket she had bought at a discount from a local store that received the "wrong" Rangers jackets. She didn't mind, though, because, as she said, "I bought if for almost nothing, and it's in the right colors" (blue and red).

From my vantage point right behind home plate, I had the chance not to see the ball a lot more clearly than I would have not seen the ball from the press box. With the early starting time, the shadows played optical havoc with the ball and, no doubt, with the eyes of the Tiger hitters. Ryan's fastballs were impressive blurs. Even though a trained eye could pick up the rotation on his curves the moment they left his hand, they immediately dropped off into the literal twilight zone halfway between the mound and the plate. I pitied the Tiger hitters, four of whom struck out in the first two innings.

Unfortunately for the fans, Ryan struggled in his Ranger debut, an assessment he himself revealed in his own grunts and "damns" on the mound, all clearly audible behind the plate. Even Ranger catcher Jim Sundberg made mention of Ryan's verbal frustrations on the hill, noting to a reporter after the game that Ryan "did a lot of yelling on the mound, more than he has done all spring."[2]

In the end, Ryan lasted five complete innings, throwing 107 pitches; he registered eight strikeouts and allowed four runs (three earned), seven hits, and three walks. The Rangers went on to win the game 5-4 when Cecil Espy scored on Raphael Palmeiro's single in the seventh inning. But Ryan did not get credited with a decision. It was not an impressive outing for the future Hall of Fame pitcher, but the fact that Nolan Ryan was out there at all impressed the fans at Arlington Stadium. "I don't care how he pitched," exclaimed one season ticket holder to his neighbor. "That's Nolan Ryan in a Texas Ranger uniform. That's ——ing unbelievable."

As Chuck Morgan, the Rangers' announcer, recalled several months later, "Even though he didn't pitch well, the crowd was on every pitch. Mike Stone was up in the booth when the game started, and after Nolan's first few pitches, I remember telling him, 'Hey, I'm paying tonight when I leave.'"

Throughout the 1989 season and beyond, Nolan Ryan continued to influence the Ranger team and to make various impressions on franchise members and fans as they came to know him, either personally or through the media.

"Nolie" as Franchise Hero

If Nolan Ryan had signed with the Los Angeles Dodgers or New York Yankees, he would have become one of many superstars in the lore of the franchise. But when he signed with the lowly Texas Rangers— the only other team besides Seattle that never had been to the playoffs in their history (at least before the Marlins and Rockies entered the league)— Ryan became an instant franchise hero.

Ryan's Impact on the Bottom Line
Although Ranger owners paid Ryan almost $15 million from 1989 through 1993, their investment was well worth it. Former president Mike Stone said that there are few individual players fans will pay to see: "You can

count them on one hand for both leagues. Nolan is one of those players."
In 1992 Ranger management expected Ryan to pay dividends even after
he retired, motivating them to sign a ten-year personal services contract
(for publicity appearances) with him that would go into effect upon his
retirement.

It is virtually impossible to assess the exact financial impact Nolan Ryan
has had on the Ranger franchise, but in an age when the business of baseball is featured prominently in media coverage, reporters have offered various estimates. When Ryan first signed with the club, one hundred twenty
new season tickets were sold within a week. As the ticket manager was
quoted by one sports columnist, "That's $85,000 in fresh revenue right
off the top."[3] During the extensive media coverage as Ryan approached
his 5,000th strikeout, one television reporter for the ABC affiliate in Dallas
exaggerated that Nolan was "directly responsible" for an increase in attendance of more than three hundred thousand, which "adds up to an additional $1.5 million for the Rangers' cash registers." At the end of the 1989
season, the Rangers' home attendance for the year surpassed 2 million
(2,043,993) for the first time in franchise history, exceeding the previous
year's 1.58 million by almost 500,000 fans. One newspaper report estimated
that this increase resulted in $2.5 million in additional revenue, attrib-
utable to Ryan, while a television report concluded boldly, if inaccurately,
"Nolan Ryan has meant the difference between profit and loss for the
Rangers."

"Sure, you can come up with a number," acknowledged John McMichael,
then Ranger controller, "but it is difficult because there are so many in-
tangibles. For example, it would be myopic to say that his financial impact was x number of fans he drew times eight dollars" (the average worth
of each fan at a game in 1989). Such a "myopic" figure would be the difference between Ryan's nineteen starts, which averaged 28,420 in attendance, and non-Ryan games, which averaged 25,067 — an average of 3,353
more fans — times his nineteen starts, for a total of 63,707 more fans and
a net total of $509,656 that can be directly attributed to Ryan in 1989.
Yet even this figure is artificially low because one of Ryan's starts was a
make-up game against the Mariners that drew only 4,654 fans, 10,000 less
than the lowest of his regular starts. Public relations director John Blake
says he simply tells reporters that Ryan accounts for 7,000–8,000 more in
attendance per start than other Ranger pitchers.

But as McMichael continued, "How many fans did he bring out that
returned five or six times to the ballpark, regardless of whether he was
pitching? Also, he drew more out-of-town fans who were a boon to hotels
and restaurants in the area, so he had a more macro impact as well." And
he concluded simply, "Coming up with a specific number is something
that I don't even do."

Stone summarized his feelings on the matter the day after Ryan's 5,000th strikeout game: "Reporters keep calling me to find out how much Ryan has meant in terms of dollars and cents, and I keep telling them that you don't measure the meaning of Nolan Ryan in terms of the bottom line. You measure him as a human being whose values of hard work, dedication, and humility stand out."

Even so, front office managers still proudly admit that signing Nolan Ryan was "a good investment," and they have been fond of saying, as Tom Grieve told reporters before the 5,000th strikeout game, that "Nolan Ryan has paid for himself."

Ryan also generated additional revenues for baseball-related businesses inside and outside the stadium. To name a few examples, one stadium store sold a record 6,000 Ryan commemorative shirts at $15 each for that August 22 game, and the Stadium Club restaurant and suites did record business on most of Ryan's starts, especially on August 22 and on the Sunday afternoon game against Boston in April, when the number of buffets served almost tripled the best day of the previous year. Another souvenir shop off stadium grounds reported that Ranger jerseys with the number "34" (Ryan's number) outsold other numbers seven-to-one, while a baseball card shop reported the price of Ryan's rookie card increased from $225 to $450 after his 5,000th strikeout. One report estimated that Ryan alone brought in $1.7 million to the local economy.

Ryan even helped unauthorized ticket scalpers turn a profit, despite a crackdown by Ranger officials and local police. As one scalper told me, "With Nolan here, it's finally possible to make some money on the Rangers."

Ryan's Impact on the Field

As noted in Chapter 1, when Ryan was signed by the Rangers, General Manager Tom Grieve told reporters: "We are not doing this for image; we are not doing this to sell tickets; we are doing this because Nolan Ryan is a pitcher who can win baseball games." In 1989 Ryan's sixteen wins were the most among Ranger pitchers (and tied for twelfth in the American League); Ryan also led Ranger pitchers in innings pitched (239.1, eighth in the A.L.), earned run average (3.20, twelfth in A.L.), and starts (thirty-two), and he was second in complete games (six). He also brought stability to the Ranger pitching staff, who had struggled in the previous few years but who, in 1989, enjoyed their best team earned run average (3.91) in six years.

In 1989 Ryan also led the major leagues with a club record 301 strikeouts, his sixth 300-strikeout season and only the twenty-second in history. He led the league in innings per start (7.48) and held the opposition to a .187 (162-867) batting average, the lowest in the majors among the seventy-five pitchers who qualified to vie for the earned run average title (with 162 or more innings pitched). He pitched a pair of complete game one-hitters and carried five no-hitters into the eighth inning or later. His efforts during the 1989 season earned him the Ranger "Pitcher of the Year Award" from the Dallas–Fort Worth baseball writers, as well as the American League's "Joe Cronin Award," given for achievement.

In 1990 Ryan again led the major leagues in strikeouts (232), and was thirteenth in earned run average (3.44); he ranked second in the club in wins (thirteen) and was third in starts (thirty) and innings (204). In 1991 he held the opposition to a major league low .173 batting average, and he was ranked third in the league in strikeouts (203) and fifth in earned run average (2.91). He led the Rangers' staff in earned run average, shutouts (two), and strikeouts, and was second in wins (twelve), starts (twenty-seven), complete games (two), and innings (173). In 1992, he ranked third on the Rangers in starts (twenty-seven), strikeouts (157), and complete games (two).

In his five years with the Rangers, Ryan was 51-39, with the second best winning percentage (.575) and the fourth lowest earned run average (3.43) in team history. More important, during this time he notched his 5,000th strikeout, his 300th win, and his sixth and seventh no-hitters— the last of which was the first by a Ranger pitcher in Arlington Stadium. A good baseball investment indeed.

Ryan's Symbolic Impact on the Franchise
Ryan has been directly responsible for increasing the visibility of a Ranger team that used to have trouble getting local media coverage in a town dominated by the Dallas Cowboys. With Ryan the Rangers received more national and local coverage than ever before. While increased local coverage was expected, the Rangers have received unprecedented and impressive national coverage—including cover stories—in *Sports Illustrated* and *The Sporting News.*[4]

Ryan's 5,000th strikeout in 1989, his 300th win and sixth no-hitter in 1990, and his seventh no-hitter in 1991 enjoyed overwhelming coverage in newspapers across the country and on national radio and television news and sports programs. "We got a lot of mileage out of the strikeout list and everything else associated with the 5,000th strikeout," John Blake said proudly. "I think a lot of it, though, had to do with Nolan, rather than just some guy with some number. I think if somebody else had been going for number 5,000, it might not have been so big a deal."

Ryan's seventh no-hitter, on May 1, 1991, overshadowed Rickie Henderson's record-breaking career steal, which occurred earlier on the same day—even on the West Coast, where Henderson's Oakland Athletics play. Ryan's picture and story appeared on the front page of the next day's *Sacramento Bee*—essentially an extended hometown paper for the Oakland A's—while Henderson's picture and story ran on the front page of the sports section. John Blake summarized the visibility that Ryan has earned: "If the average fan in North Dakota couldn't name a Ranger player before 1989, he now can at least name Nolan Ryan."

Ryan's presence on the team may have been more important symbolically in terms of the credibility he brought to the franchise. After all, the Rangers do not have a very glorious history, and the team's image around the league and around the country has not shone very brightly in past years. The franchise improved its image in the late 1980s with the development of an outstanding minor league system, which has produced highly touted young players like Ruben Sierra, Juan Gonzalez, and Ivan Rodriguez, but the signing of Ryan brought additional — and immediate — credibility.

When Ryan signed as a free agent, sportswriters in the area and across the country were unanimous in their praise of the Rangers' decision to sign him. Randy Galloway, who had been fond of criticizing the Ranger franchise, wrote that Ryan's move to the Rangers "was the crowning touch to a positive image blast that the Rangers have received during the last three days of the [1988] baseball winter meetings."[5] The fact that Ryan would sign with the Rangers in the first place was important. The director of sales and broadcasting said, "It gives the franchise credibility that a man of his baseball stature would want to play here." Dave Fendrick, the director of promotions, said simply that "with Nolan Ryan, we know we're in the big leagues."

Ryan's Personal Impact on Members of the Franchise
Although Ryan's signing helped the franchise itself, we must remember that "the franchise" consists of many different individuals, all of whom have been affected by Ryan in various ways. "He lifts your image up to his level," said Dave Fendrick, "and brings the franchise image up to his level. I'm just privileged to be around the guy. That's how I look at it. He makes my job easier, too, because he helps the organization command that much more respect by him being on the team."

Ryan made a number of front office and ballpark jobs easier to accomplish. For example, it was much easier to sell tickets and advertisements with Ryan than it had been without him. Chuck Morgan was quoted in one column telling about the response he received when he called the president of a local company to buy program advertisements before and after the Rangers signed Ryan:

> I say to his secretary, "Hi, I'm Chuck Morgan from the Rangers." And she said, "Do you really admit to that?" After I picked myself up off the floor, I said, "I want to discuss with him buying an ad in next season's program." She said, "I can assure you right now he's *not* interested." That same seretary called back this week. The company president purchased a full-page program ad for $8,500. Thank you very much, Nolan Ryan.[6]

Ryan also helped the franchise in hiring part-time seasonal workers, as the number of workers returning and the number of new applications increased dramatically after his signing. "There was no way that I wasn't gonna work out here this year with Nolan Ryan pitching," said a returning parking lot attendant. "He's awesome."

In other ways, though, Ryan's presence made some jobs more challenging. Employees in the media relations department have had to write about Ryan's many, many accomplishments for the media guide, press releases, program articles, and other printed materials. Perhaps the largest media relations task was preparing a list of every one of Ryan's strikeout victims as he approached his 5,000th strikeout. This task was assigned to Larry Kelly, the director of publications, who examined game sheets from every one of Ryan's innings pitched since 1966. The list took Kelly over a hundred hours to compile and check. "It took a lot of work and was kind of a pain," he said, "but it's fun looking up stuff about Nolan. He's a living legend." The night of Ryan's 5,000th strikeout, the late Bart Giamatti, then baseball commissioner and former president of Yale University, scanned the list and told Kelly, "Son, if you had done that at Yale, you would be a Ph.D."

Joe Macko, the Rangers' clubhouse manager, had to be especially careful with Ryan's uniform, which was potentially valuable. "We have to be really careful when we go on the road," he explained. "We don't even put his name on his bag because somebody might steal it to get his shirt. I generally put his uniform in my bag when we travel; then I take it out and put it in his locker." One unknown intruder did steal Ryan's jersey after his debut at Arlington Stadium, prompting Macko to keep it locked up until just before game time for future games.

Finally, while employees always are hounded with requests for complimentary tickets throughout the year, requests for Ryan's starts—especially for his 5,000th strikeout game in 1989 and his unsuccessful attempt to win his 300th game at Arlington Stadium in 1990—put even more strain on front office employees. "I have ended a few friendships with people who wanted tickets for Ryan's games," admitted stadium director Mat Stolley. "You just get so tired of dealing with requests, and I didn't handle some well. I can only accommodate so many people anyway, but for Nolan, they come out of the woodwork."

Since he debuted in 1989, different employees have developed their own personal views of the "meaning" of Nolan Ryan related to the perspective of their positions. "After doing the research on Nolan for the media guide," John Blake said, "I realized that I was probably dealing with the top athlete that I'll ever work with in my career. I don't know for sure, but I can't imagine working with anyone more special than Nolan Ryan."

Chuck Morgan put it this way: "Personally, it's just such a thrill to say, 'And number 34, Nolan Ryan.' My biggest thrill in baseball was to say,

'Ladies and gentlemen, with that strikeout, Nolan Ryan becomes the first player in baseball history to strike out 5,000.' No one probably heard it since the crowd was cheering in unknown decibels, but it was a thrill for me. I haven't had butterflies like that since I played athletics."

Mat Stolley gave his perspectives: "We watch so many games up in the command post, and sometimes when I'm up there, it's a dog game against a dog team, and there isn't a whole lot of interest in the game. But every time Nolan pitched last year, I got excited. He made me a fan again. After watching so many games, there aren't many players who make you a fan again."

Ranger owner George W. Bush recalled several moments when Ryan was on the mound that first season, especially his 5,000th strikeout. But Bush remembered the home run that Bo Jackson hit off Ryan with special fondness: "The circumstances were such that Bo had faced Nolan four times in Kansas City, and he struck him out all four. Nolan said he just threw heat. Bo then comes to Texas and the first two times at the plate, Nolan strikes him out. So when Bo comes up again, the crowd is all over him and Nolan, as I remember, brushes him back—which I would assume is one of the most frightening experiences a person can go through—and then Bo hits an unbelievable blast. I want to say it was 468 feet or something like that. He hit it so hard and so loud that the place went from heckling to just shock. It was an unbelievable moment."[7]

Perhaps Jay Miller, the director of stadium administration, put it best when he told this story to the stadium manager and the director of security just a few days after Ryan's 5,000th strikeout: "You won't believe what I got today. I got a plant from Nolan for my office with a note thanking me for getting him extra tickets for his 5,000th strikeout game. I couldn't believe it. He didn't have to do that." He turned to me and explained, "Most players expect you to get them the tickets, and they wouldn't think about thanking you. There aren't many people you can say this about, but Nolan is the closest thing to a hero that we have in this profession."

Presenting Ryan in the Texas Media

The Texas sports media really had no choice but to cover Ryan extensively during his tenure with the Rangers. Ryan was a well-known sports figure, and his move to the Rangers and his accomplishments there were newsworthy events. Still, members of the media made a variety of choices about how to cover Ryan.

Helping Us Know Him
When Ryan was signed by the Rangers, a flurry of reports detailed the efforts by Ranger officers, celebrated the actual signing, chronicled the

career history of the pitcher, and speculated on his potential impact on the franchise. Many of these reports informed readers and viewers about the personal side of Ryan. Before his first season with Texas, one lengthy article in the society pages of the *Dallas Morning News* depicted his early years as a boy in rural Alvin, Texas, and gave readers such tidbits as his nickname ("Express"), his favorite music ("country-western"), his personal transportation ("a pickup"), his hero ("John Wayne"), and the worst job he ever had ("unloading boxcars in a lumber yard during the summers when [he] was in high school").[8] A year later the same newspaper told of Ryan's experience growing up with undiagnosed dyslexia, quoting Ryan, "When I had that, they didn't diagnose it as that. It was frustrating and embarrassing. I could tell you a lot of horror stories about what you feel like on the inside."[9] Television news regularly reported on aspects of Ryan's life on and off the mound and also showed Ryan himself, pitching on the mound, riding horseback on his cattle ranch, and talking about his career.

Whether or not these reports, especially those about Ryan's favorite music and his pickup truck, are newsworthy may be subject to debate. However, as Tracy Ringolsby explained in an interview, "It doesn't matter how many questions I've asked him and how many times I've heard answers that sound the same, I have to find something new about Nolan Ryan because the public wants to know *everything* about him. It's my job to help them get to know Nolan Ryan through my reports."

Researchers who study the mass media suggest that audiences use such information to develop "para-social relationships" and to engage in "para-social interaction" with valued others whom the audience members would not likely know directly. "All this detailed information," wrote two sports sociologists, "enables the devotee to identify more closely with the team and to develop imaginary-intimate relationships with the players."[10]

Whether or not sportswriters and sportscasters intend for audiences to use this information to develop such para-social relationships, the choice to report such information makes these relationships likely. So when country music blared from the Arlington Stadium speakers between innings at one of Ryan's starts, one fan could tell his ballpark neighbor, "That's Nolie's favorite type of music."

Interestingly, through newspaper and television reports on Ryan, readers and viewers also got to know members of the Ranger franchise a little better. For example, the coverage of the 5,000th strikeout not only included game highlights and quotes from Ryan, but also chronicled the activities of Ranger personnel as they prepared for the game. Audiences learned that stadium administrator Jay Miller had been called for jury duty that week but that he arranged a deal with a bailiff—a reprieve from jury duty in exchange for an autographed ball. And they learned that media relations assistant Larry Kelly had spent several weeks prior to the game compiling the list of Ryan's strikeout victims.

"Expressing" Ryan through Metaphor

Reporters and sportscasters have used a variety of colorful expressions and images to characterize Ryan and his career. Sports reporters have more poetic license to use metaphor and colorful language than do news reporters. These metaphors and images shape the perception of sports for various audiences, and they have played a role in shaping our experience of Nolan Ryan.

One of the most common images used by the Texas media to characterize Ryan directs attention to his Texas roots and residency. "Ryan *is* Texas," Dallas sportswriter Phil Rogers told me in an interview, "and our readers are Texas. It's the perfect match." Former Ranger pitching coach Tom House put it this way: "Nolie is the essence of Texas mentality. He's bigger than life—on and off the field."[11]

Because of his rural Texas roots, reporters have used metaphors from the mythic West to embellish their coverage of Ryan. For example, when Ryan had his first matchup against fastball pitcher and native Texan Roger Clemens of the Boston Red Sox on a Sunday afternoon in 1989, members of the Texas media predictably cast the matchup as a classic, if cliché-ridden, western drama. That night, the weekend sports anchor for the Dallas ABC affiliate framed his report in terms of the imagery and mythology of the Texas frontier: "The fans came to see a duel, a showdown like the ones that used to take place in the early days of Texas. The good guys, wearing white, led by a feared gunslinger named Nolan Ryan. . . . The bad guys in dark were led by Roger Clemens, a transplanted Texan who's now the fastest gun in the East." The next day, a *Dallas Morning News* headline described the game as the "duel of gunslingers." It was Texas at "high noon."

Philosophers George Lakoff and Mark Johnson have argued that metaphor is one of the most powerful forms we use to experience our social world. "It is as though the ability to comprehend experience through metaphor were a sense, like seeing or touching or hearing, with metaphors providing the only way to perceive and experience much of the world," they wrote. "Metaphor is as much a part of our functioning as our sense of touch, and as precious."[12]

For sports fans metaphors in the sports pages are as much a part of our morning experience as are cups of coffee. For Nolan Ryan fans, the metaphors used by sportswriters and sportscasters reinforced their sense of Ryan as the embodiment of the western myth—a myth that will always sell very well in Texas. In this way the Texas media have presented images of Texas through Ryan, helping to sell newspapers and increase viewership in Texas markets. By using these images from the mythic West, the media also established a mythological aspect to Ryan's status as an American sports hero, a theme developed in the next chapter.

Creating History: Covering Ryan's 5,000th Strikeout

When Nolan Ryan approached and then registered his 5,000th strikeout in 1989 against Rickie Henderson of the Oakland Athletics, the media presented the event as an important historic occasion. As noted briefly in the last chapter, for non-baseball-oriented observers, the game was the epitome of a "pseudo-event" since Ryan already had the major league record for strikeouts, and every additional strikeout was a new milestone. But as baseball reporters and sabermetricians interpreted it, the unprecedented plateau of 5,000 strikeouts merited special attention.

Members of the media presented the game as historic in many ways. NBC, ABC, and CBS featured stories about the Ryan milestone on their national newscasts, and many newspapers around the country featured it on the front page. The three newspapers in the Dallas–Fort Worth area provided special Ryan inserts with full-page color posters, K signs, and stories about the game from every angle. The media presented Ryan's 5,000th strikeout on the same level as other "great records in baseball history," such as Joe DiMaggio's 56-game hitting streak, Pete Rose's 4,256 career hits, Hank Aaron's 755 career home runs, and Lou Gehrig's 2,130 consecutive games played. Dallas writer Gerry Fraley indicated that with 5,000 strikeouts, Ryan had 29 percent more strikeouts than Walter Johnson's previous high mark of 3,508; he contrasted this with other baseball records, showing that Pete Rose's 4,256 hits were merely a 1.5 percent edge over Ty Cobb's 4,191 hits, and Hank Aaron's 755 home runs were merely 5 percent above Babe Ruth's 714 homers.[13]

Reporters quoted veteran baseball managers such as Sparky Anderson, Whitey Herzog, and Tom Lasorda and famous players such as Reggie Jackson, Tom Seaver, and Jim Palmer to corroborate the historic nature of Ryan's milestone. Sparky Anderson said: "We're looking at a record that will never be touched. Nobody will ever have the power at his age that he does." Another report quoted baseball statistician Bill James as saying, "The language has no words to describe something like this. It's unbelievable."[14]

The media also used comments of fans in attendance to describe the event in historic terms. The front page of the *Dallas Times Herald* quoted nine-year-old David Wyrick of Waco, Texas, who said, "I'll probably tell my grandchildren it was the most exciting thing that ever happened in my life." A forty-one-year-old woman named Diana Inge was quoted as saying, "I'm a history person. I read history and to know that I'm going to see history is a thrill. The gods have shined on me."[15]

Finally, the media reported that the president of the United States himself, who was vacationing in Maine, would be watching the game. Reports indicated that President Bush received permission from Home Sports Entertainment, the cable network that covered the game live, to descramble the signal, even though HSE was not authorized by Major League Baseball to televise games in Maine. But the HSE general manager was quoted as saying, "We hope that if we get in trouble, we'll be able to get a presidential pardon."[16]

Through the Texas media, the event was presented as a historic one not only for Ryan, but also for Arlington Stadium itself, the site of very few historic baseball occurrences—especially for the home team. Tom Grieve told reporters in the dugout before the 5,000th strikeout game, "Arlington Stadium hasn't seen this kind of excitement since David Clyde started his first game for the Rangers right out of high school." In short the Texas media presented "their" hometown pitcher as a historic hero and "their" hometown field as a historic site in baseball lore.

Picking Ryan Sound Bites for Broadcast
Television reports showed us the reactions of Nolan Ryan before, during, and after the historic game. Their coverage used clips from Ryan's press conference the day before the game and especially from his conference immediately after the game. CNN "Sports Night" even carried part of the press conference live, joining it just as ABC correspondent Dick Schaap asked Ryan how long his right arm was. (Ryan answered that his sleeve length is thirty-five inches.) But television sports coverage from national organizations such as ESPN and CNN, as well as coverage from local Dallas–Fort Worth affiliates, used few "sound bites" from his post-game press conference. Although Ryan made an initial statement and answered twenty-seven questions in his fifteen-minute session, television stations used clips from only eight of his answers.[17] (A transcript of Ryan's post-game press conference is presented in Appendix A.)

Two sound bites were used in television reports more than any others. The first was Ryan's answer to a question about his nervousness before the game: "I was very nervous today. In fact, coming down the interstate, I drove right by the ballpark, to show you where my mind was. I had to turn around and come back." The second clip was from his response to a question about his frustration at not getting the record earlier: "I heard that before the game those guys [the Athletics] had a pool about who it was gonna be and I'm sure none of them wanted to be number 5,000. I'm sure Rickie [Henderson] didn't."

The decision of television news editors to use these two quotes more than any others again reveals the potential function of the media to help fans develop para-social relationships with sports figures. The quotes used most often in video reports were related to Ryan's personal feelings and emotions. In the first quote, Ryan disclosed his nervousness about the game; in the second, he speculated on the feelings of his opponents (not wanting to be number 5,000) and also revealed insider knowledge about their private clubhouse "pool." The only other clip that was used more than once was Ryan's description of a private conversation he had with his 5,000th victim, Rickie Henderson, immediately after the game. Thus, the media provided viewers with vicarious access to events in the behind-the-scenes areas of clubhouses and dugouts, as well as information that helped them relate to the historic sports figure as a real person with human emotions.

The Diamond Vision television screen at Arlington Stadium also had an important media function on that night. Videotapes of all of Ryan's milestone strikeouts from the past were played, as was a taped message from President Bush to Ryan. "Congratulations, Nolan Ryan," Bush said on the big center field screen. "What an amazing accomplishment. Indeed, everybody that loves baseball pays tribute to you on this very special record-breaking occasion. Well done, my friend. Well done, my noble friend."

And when Ryan struck out Henderson for number 5,000, the Diamond Vision showed not only the live action of the field, as players ran to congratulate Ryan, but also the live action in the stands, as fans cheered loudly and showed *K* signs. Ballpark fans could watch Nolan Ryan on the field, as well as themselves, cheering Ryan together, in the stands. In this way, the ballpark television stressed the fans' involvement in the celebration of the historic event, and it reinforced a rich sense of a united ballpark community.

The following year, the same Diamond Vision screen at Arlington Stadium broadcast live coverage of Ryan's 300th win from County Stadium in Milwaukee. More than 10,000 Rangers fans watched television together at the ballpark as Ryan achieved his milestone victory.

Experiencing the Ryan Express at the Ballpark

On that night in August, 1989, and throughout Ryan's seasons as a Ranger, fans and workers at the ballpark experienced the meaning of Nolan Ryan in different ways. Ryan united fans in a way that promoted their identification with the Rangers and their integration into the Arlington Stadium community. Every time Ryan pitched at Arlington Stadium, fans revealed and shared their knowledge about his various baseball accomplishments and his personal qualities. A middle-aged man wearing a Sony Walkman quizzed his ballpark neighbor, "Did you know that Ryan and Koufax are the only two guys to average a strikeout an inning?" At a game with the Royals, a young man told his wife, "Hey, Ryan's first no-hitter was against Kansas City, so maybe he'll get another one tonight." A young boy told his mother, "Oh wow, Mom, it says here [in the program] that Nolan Ryan was born on my birthday" (January 31).

After the list of Ryan's strikeouts was released during the week of his 5,000th strikeout, fans joined together as they playfully taunted California Angel batter Claudell Washington, who had struck out against Ryan more than any other batter (thirty-seven times at that point). And when Ryan lost no-hitters in the eighth and ninth inning on two occasions at Arlington Stadium in 1989, two different people—one a fan and one an usher—made essentially identical statements of, "There goes a million bucks for Little League." (In celebration of its fiftieth anniversary, Little League Baseball had been promised $1.25 million by Best Western Hotels and American Express if Ryan, a former Little League player, registered his sixth no-hitter during the 1989 season. Unfortunately for Little League Baseball, Ryan notched his sixth no-hitter the next season.)

Sharing Ryan Signs and Symbols
Fans and workers also shared in the display and consumption of other symbols that revealed their identification with Ryan in the ballpark. At Ryan's first start as a Ranger, several groups of fans posted *K* signs in the ballpark, a rarely performed ritual in Arlington Stadium history. Most fans know that the letter *K* is the symbol for a strikeout, and to display them around the stadium reveals knowledge of the symbol and of its appropriateness for the strikeout leader.

However, not everyone in the stands shared in an understanding of this symbolic ritual, as Della Britton, the secretary of stadium operations, revealed in a story she told to the stadium manager: "This older lady just came up to me in personal services and said she wanted to file a complaint that the Ku Klux Klan was demonstrating in the ballpark. I said, 'You're not a regular baseball fan, are you?' She said, 'No, not really.' I told her, 'Ma'am, the letter *K* stands for a strikeout, and right now Nolan has three strikeouts so there are three *K*'s in the stands. The minute he gets his fourth strikeout, you'll see another *K* go up.' Poor lady."

A variety of other symbols relating to Ryan were displayed throughout the year, helping to integrate the ballpark community of fans and workers. For every Ryan start, signs were placed in the stands, such as "Texas RyanGers," "Ryan Express," and "5000." The Ranger franchise produced certificates commemorating Ryan's 5,000th strikeout and made them available to fans free of charge so they could have a ceremonial space to display their ticket stubs from the 5,000th strikeout game. The certificate read: "This certificate of recognition is given to those who were in attendance August 22, 1989. Oakland Athletics Vs. Texas Rangers. Your enthusiasm and support have played a major role in helping to achieve this milestone."

HSE, the cable company that has broadcast Ranger home games over the years, sponsored a "Ryan 5,000 Poster Night," during which all in attendance received a poster of an artist's conception of Ryan throwing the

5,000th strikeout pitch. Such mementos displayed the relative integration through Ryan of—and the commodification of Ryan for—the ballpark community.

On the other hand, not all Ryan symbols have been used by ballpark audiences to integrate community. Some have been used by particular groups to define and mark more segregated communities. When Ryan made his very first start, about three hundred people from his home town of Alvin, Texas, attended the game and wore "Ryan Express" buttons as they sat in one full section of the stadium marked off by "Alvin to Arlington" signs. On that historic August night in 1989, ARA Services, the company that runs food and drink concessions at Arlington Stadium, handed out special Ryan buttons to its employees as gifts but warned them that they would be fired if they sold their buttons. Media credentials issued on that night were special symbols of the reporters' access to restricted areas of the ballpark and were treated by reporters as unique mementos of the game. "Those people out there may have their tickets for souvenirs," bragged one reporter in the auxiliary press box to a colleague, "but we can hang our press passes on the wall and tell our kids that we *covered* his 5,000th."

"Where Were You When Nolan Did It"?

Many people participated in the festive rituals of cheering, talking, and symbol-sharing on the night Ryan registered his 5,000th strikeout, but stories about that event were shared through the remainder of the season and are still told to this day. The most common question after the milestone strikeout game was "Where were you when Nolan did it?" It was a question that everyone in attendance could answer without hesitation. As I interviewed ballpark workers in the days and weeks following the 5,000th strikeout, every worker answered the question quickly and in great detail. In a strange way, their stories about where they were when Ryan "did it" were similar to the accounts of people who were living at the time of the assassination of John F. Kennedy, a point noted by Rangers' announcer Chuck Morgan. "Working for the Texas Rangers that night," he said, "was like a John Kennedy type experience. I mean, everybody knows what they were doing when Nolan Ryan struck out his 5,000th."

ARA personnel director Erika Link remembered it this way: "I was standing by Section 212, and I looked around, and all the stand workers in the section were standing behind me. They saw me and said, 'Oh, we're sorry, we'll get back to the stand.' I said, 'Hey, don't worry about it, no one is up there anyway.'"

Bob Garvey, who was running the radar gun behind home plate that night, told his story: "I was so glad that he did it with a 96 mile-per-hour fastball and not a 92 or 93 mile-per-hour one. It was so intense down there. I was charting the pitches and handing the sheet to [an assistant]. I was also wired up to HSE and was trying to talk into this box to give them the pitches. I didn't even see the flashbulbs going off in the stadium." He sighed and repeated himself, "It was so intense."

Two security guards who monitored gates behind the outfield fences remembered the strikeout in different ways. Espy Randolph, the guard who monitors the grounds crew gate, normally listens to the game on the AM radio he bought for $1.99 at a local thrift shop. For the Ryan strikeout, though, he sneaked in to watch the historic moment from a vantage point under the outfield stands. "Don't tell my supervisor," he joked with me, "but it was pretty quiet back there, and I just had to look over that fence to watch him do it."

Tom Mullarkey, the guard who monitors the gate to the visiting clubhouse, however, could not sneak a peek into the stadium because he was trying to keep people from hanging on the barbed-wire fence to see the action on the field through the small space between the left field bleachers and the lower infield seats. "If I would have gone in to watch," Mullarkey told me, "there would have been at least fifty people crashing through this gate. So I listened to it on the radio. But I ordered this shirt today that says I was there for Ryan's 5,000th."

Not surprisingly, Ryan's seventh no-hitter, in 1991, was remembered in the same way. Like the 5,000th strikeout, the seventh no-hitter depended on one moment—on one pitch. But in the case of Ryan's seventh no-hitter, the tension lasted the entire game. "Nolan was so 'on' in the first inning," remembered stadium manager Mat Stolley, "which is unusual for him. So I knew something special might happen that night. But when it started getting close after the sixth, seventh innings, I couldn't even sit down. I was pacing back and forth in the command post. I must have lost ten pounds just watching him do it." Secretary Della Britton recalled the moment when it ended: "The thing I remember the most is when he smiled at [catcher] Mike Stanley when Stanley rushed the mound to shake his hand. I think Nolan realized what had happened at that exact moment." Fittingly, the secretary has a picture of "that exact moment" on the wall in her office.

Veteran Dallas sportswriter Blackie Sherrod published his remembrance of Ryan's seventh no-hitter. Sherrod was holed up in a Louisville hotel room with several gray-haired members of the "senior circuit" of sportswriters who were covering the Kentucky Derby. One of the writers received a call from his office that Ryan had a no-hitter going. According to Sherrod, the writers immediately rushed to a television set and found the game. "Bent backs straightened and leaned forward, sagging lids lifted, cigarettes were forgotten, and nary a word was uttered as the fogies stared unblinking at Ryan throwing the last two innings of his seventh no-hit game."[18]

Although the moments during that August night in 1989 and that May night in 1991 were fleeting, the memories are relived in the stories of ballpark workers and fans who watched Nolan do it. Their stories were shared with a variety of audiences at the time, and they will continue to be shared with future generations of ballpark fans and workers, ensuring that Ryan's significance to the Texas Rangers will be lasting.

These stories about Ryan, especially those presented in the media, also extend his meaning to people outside of Arlington Stadium. After all, while Nolan Ryan has special significance to members and fans of the Ranger franchise, his meaning in American culture transcends any one franchise. For some, he is a genuine sports hero. For others, he is a star celebrity and a profitable commodity. For still others, he represents a preferred image of American masculinity. In the next few chapters, I examine how these and other meanings of Nolan Ryan have been reinforced in the mass media.

A Hero for All Ages

"Heroes are for comic books and dreams. But not always. Anyone heard anything bad lately about Nolan Ryan?"

—USA Today

"From work habits that have kept his middle-aged muscles fighting trim, to a clean-cut personal life straight out of the rural Texas he loves, Mr. Ryan is a hero for all ages."

—Dallas Morning News

"Nolan Ryan (He's a Hero to Us All)"

—Jerry Jeff Walker

3

Most baseball fans would agree that Nolan Ryan is a genuine sports hero. As noted in the last chapter, members of the Texas Rangers consider Ryan a franchise hero—when he first signed with the Rangers, some even called him a franchise savior. As noted in Chapter 1, many sportswriters also called Ryan a hero, especially in his later years as the "ageless wonder" and "miracle man." But what exactly is a hero? In a media age when salaries and scandals receive as much coverage as scores and seasons and when anyone who does something out of the ordinary is called a hero for a day, does the label really mean anything anymore? This chapter considers these questions and examines how the mass media represented Nolan Ryan as a sports—and an American—hero.

The Hero in Contemporary Society

In ancient times the hero was a mythological figure who possessed attributes of great stature (such as strength, bravery, or magic) and who performed acts of great significance (such as discovering brave new worlds, parting seas, or killing fire-breathing dragons). Heroes were thought to be favored by the gods and were often deified by members of the culture. Stories and legends about the hero were passed on from generation to generation, and the hero, even more in death than in life, remained an exalted figure in the culture's history.[1]

For better or—more likely—for worse, the mediated hero in contemporary society possesses far less stature and performs acts of far less significance than the mythological hero of ancient times. Today's heroes are neither exalted nor deified, but are seen as being more down to earth. In fact, sociologist Orrin Klapp has written that many types of individuals have the potential to be contemporary heroes, including winners (the strong man, the brain, the smart operator, or the great lover), splendid performers (the showman, the players, or the playboy), heroes of social acceptability (the pin-up, the charmer, the good fellow, and the conformist), independent spirits (the bohemian, the jester, the angry communicator), and group servants (the defender, the martyr, or the benefactor). According to Klapp, even the "anti-hero" can be interpreted as a heroic figure who "seduces" audiences to challenge societal values.[2]

Although Klapp and others have suggested that many potential types of heroes exist in contemporary society, most observers agree that true heroes are individuals who have accomplished acts with important and lasting cultural significance. The contemporary hero is understood to be, as Daniel Boorstin explained, "a human figure—real or imaginary or both—who has shown greatness in some achievements." In other words, the hero "is a man or woman of great deeds."[3] The true hero is not merely an entertainer or a great performer for a day, but is someone whose greatness has withstood the test of time.

Most observers also agree that the true hero symbolizes the cultural ideals of a given society. As many suggest, the hero is a moral character who reflects and reaffirms values that are considered positive in a society. Such heroes can be used as models through which members of a culture understand and integrate themselves into the social structure of their society. Klapp argued that the dominant influences in any society, such as religion, school, the family, the government, and the mass media, use heroic models to "recruit, train, and control members of the society in accordance with these models."[4]

Though heroes themselves are individuals, the process by which these persons are understood to be heroic is interactive. The process of hero construction, as described by Henry Fairlie, is two-way: "We choose the hero. He [or she] is fit to be chosen."[5] So while it is natural to focus attention on the individual who is seen as heroic, it also is important to notice the processes by which members of the culture—particularly members of the mass media—identify the hero and share in their heroism.

Klapp even suggested that when members of society aspire to the ideals represented by a hero, they establish a "yearning relationship" in which they "get away" from themselves by "wishing or imagining" themselves to be like someone they admire.[6] In this way, members of a culture define the hero and, usually through the mass media, participate vicariously in their acts of heroism.

Sports heroes, like other heroes, are models for integration and socialization, reinforcing the culturally approved ideals of their sports and their societies. "Athletic hero worship has been accepted and even encouraged," wrote Garry Smith, "because sport represents major cultural values." Many sportswriters recall the "golden age" of sports, before the advent of television, when these sports heroes were commonplace—heroes such as Joe Louis, Knute Rockne, Lou Gehrig, Joe DiMaggio, and Jackie Robinson. "In the pre-television era," wrote Benjamin Rader, "heroes populated the world of sports." However, most observers of American culture agree that in the post-television era there are very few heroes in general, and even fewer sports heroes in particular, to serve as models in society.[7]

From Hero to Celebrity

In his classic book *The Image,* Daniel Boorstin asserted that true heroes (including sports heroes) have been in short supply for many years. Boorstin, like Klapp, suggested that although the media have given us the capability to communicate the heroic deeds of individuals to more members of society than ever before, the media have contributed to the decline of the true hero. There are several reasons for this apparent irony.

First, Boorstin wrote that there is so much media coverage of so many individuals that "the titanic figure is now only one of thousands." Since the mass media can (and do on a regular basis) make anyone well-known, those who perform large-scale acts ultimately stand only a few column inches taller than those whose actions are much smaller. As Richard Crepeau wrote about sports heroes, "Too many teams, too many players, too many events, and too much coverage have produced two extremes, the blandness of the mass and a preoccupation with the unusual or bizarre."[8]

Second, while there is too much coverage of too many individuals, there also is too much coverage of particular individuals. Crepeau put it this way: "The public figure, it seems, is continually being probed from within and without, and . . . no one can survive this sort of scrutinizing without finally being trivialized. The sheer volume of such treatment becomes overwhelming, and the world of imagination, where heroes are born and where they live and move freely, is ultimately denied expression and buried in a blizzard of data." For example, we read about the mundane practices of our sports figures, including how fast they drive, how much they sleep, and what cereals they eat for breakfast—in fact, they are sometimes on the cereal box itself. Despite the distribution of mass quantities of information about our favorite players, Crepeau argued that "ironically, we probably know as little about sports heroes today as we knew about them in earlier times. The difference is only in what kinds of things we know. What has revelatory journalism really revealed beyond titillation for a voyeuristic age? The myth of the flawed perhaps."[9]

Third, there is too much negative coverage of sports figures in a society where media managers and reporters have developed a taste for sensa-tional, conflict-oriented stories that are dramatic and attract higher reader-ship and viewership. The meanness that Joseph Wood Krutch argued many years ago had come to dominate our culture certainly dominates many of our sports columns today. While the sports media of the past ignored the off-the-field quirks and neuroses of such heroes as the womanizing, alcohol-abusing Babe Ruth, the sports media of today seem preoccupied with the search for such material. Garry Smith concluded, "It seems that the mass media which once pandered to athletic heroes now is contribut-ing to their decanonization, if not their decline."[10]

These reasons have led many writers to conclude that the celebrity is re-placing the hero in contemporary American society. As Boorstin explained, "The hero was distinguished by his achievement; the celebrity by his im-age or trademark. The hero created himself; the celebrity is created by the media. The hero was a big man; the celebrity is a big name." Unfor-tunately, as Boorstin lamented, "We can fabricate fame, we can at will (though usually at considerable expense) make a man or woman well known; but we cannot make him great. We can make a celebrity, but we can never make a hero." We can, however, make a hero seem to be less great.[11]

Although many writers point to the demise of the hero as a negative consequence of the mass media in society, Crepeau argued that the evolu-tion of American life may have eliminated the place for overarching cul-tural heroes who were needed in the past. "No longer is it possible or necessary to have heroes who appeal to all classifications of people," he said. "Now, heroes have only partial appeal to certain segments of society. As there is no unified system of values, there are no universal heroes." Crepeau suggested optimistically that the demise of the universal hero underscores the maturation of American society and "could indicate greater security of identity for Americans as a people, and therefore a willingness to accept differences and reject the bygone prejudices of one-hundred-percent Americanism." Even so, he concluded with the foreboding possi-bility that "it may be that rather than hero worship, this envy of celebrity is all that remains for a society that has lost its sense of shared values."[12]

Heroes may be in short supply, not only because there are fewer great individuals in contemporary society, but also because the mass media de-vote as much time to the mundane activities of famous celebrities as to the outstanding accomplishments of genuine heroes. With respect to pro-fessional sports, the media present few athletes who reflect the ideals of society while presenting far more athletes interested only in their own marketability. And it seems that sports audiences often are less interested in the heroic performances of individuals than in discovering the salaries of sports celebrities to gauge the value of a home team victory. Finally, I agree with Garry Smith and others that the modern day sports hero is "an endangered species."

If the sports hero is such an endangered species, then students of the game should search for those rare heroic individuals left in the wilds of professional sports. And when they are found, we should examine how the mass media represent particular athletes as sports heroes. There is no doubt that the sports media have elevated Nolan Ryan as such a hero.

Presenting Nolan Ryan as a Sports Hero

The sports media have established Nolan Ryan as a sports hero in several ways. They represented his accomplishments as great feats. They showed us that he has passed the test of time. They presented his commitment to many traditional ideals of American culture. And they elected not to publish or sensationalize negative stories about his life on and off the field.

Accomplishments and Great Feats

Ryan's accomplishments on the field are impressive, especially to fans who understand the game by the numbers. In sports the quantification of players' performances allows reporters (and fans) to comment on the historic nature of certain players or performances. Reporters certainly have commented on Ryan's achievements. Through the 1993 season, Ryan had set or tied more than fifty major league records. Ryan has several career and single-season records related to no-hitters, one-hitters, and strikeouts. He has beaten every team in both leagues (before the Colorado Rockies and Florida Marlins entered the National League in 1993), and he is one of only five pitchers to post one hundred wins in both leagues. The media reminded us before the 1993 season that among active pitchers, Ryan was first in wins, strikeouts, innings pitched, shutouts, and starts.

Ryan has earned some major league records of a more dubious nature as well. Through 1993 he had set a major league career record for bases on balls (2,795) and for wild pitches (277), and he held the record for the most years leading the major leagues in these categories. His career highs of 204 walks in 1977 and 207 walks in 1974 were the second and third highest single-season totals, just behind Bob Feller's 208 in 1938. Ryan held the record for the most years leading the American League in errors (four). And despite his lengthy career of twenty-five years, he never won a Cy Young Award for pitcher of the year, a Golden Glove Award for the best fielding pitcher, or a triple crown in pitching (most wins, most strikeouts, best earned run average). And after more than twenty-five seasons of major league baseball, he had been an All-Star just eight times.

In addition, some of Ryan's major league records are somewhat artificial. Consider these major league records—really "pseudo-records"—set by Ryan which are listed in the Rangers' media guide: fewest pitches for inning with three strikeouts (nine); most strikeouts in two consecutive games and three consecutive games; most consecutive starts without a relief appearance; and most fielding chances accepted by a pitcher in five-game series.

Ryan's strikeout numbers constitute the bulk of his major league records, and they have been ceremoniously reported by the sports media. In fact, through the 1993 season, nineteen of his fifty-plus major league records were related to career and single-season strikeouts. Ryan's 383 strikeouts in 1973 are a major league record, and he owns five of the top eight single-season strikeout totals since 1900. His six seasons with 300 or more strikeouts, his fifteen seasons with 200 or more strikeouts, and his twenty-four seasons with 100 or more strikeouts are also records. He has averaged 9.55 strikeouts per nine innings to become one of only two pitchers with a career average of one strikeout an inning per nine innings. (The other was Sandy Koufax, with 9.28 every nine innings.) He has fanned 15 or more in a game 26 times and 10 or more 215 times, both records. Through the 1993 season, Ryan had fanned 1,176 different players, including eight father-son combinations, twelve sets of brothers, and twenty-one members of the Hall of Fame.

But are strikeouts truly great baseball feats? Although many sportswriters and baseball fans have been amazed by his numbers, Ryan's reported preoccupation with obtaining these strikeouts has also been the subject of media criticism. "I've had mixed emotions about Nolan," admitted Hall of Fame pitcher Jim Palmer on the occasion of Ryan's 5,000th strikeout. "I thought he dwelled on strikeouts too much. But I played on much better teams and didn't need strikeouts to win." In the same article, Bob Feller offered similar criticism: "Strikeouts are easier to get now. In my time, hitters were embarrassed to strike out, especially against a power pitcher. . . . It's different now. Players don't care about striking out."[13] In retrospect, this criticism from these two Hall of Fame pitchers makes them appear jealous of the attention Ryan has received for his strikeout records. Indeed, the importance of Ryan's strikeout records has been grossly inflated by the massive media coverage of each milestone strikeout. Sportswriter Tom Boswell admitted the tendency of reporters to inflate the importance of baseball records: "Those of us who cover sports have perfected the saturation reportage of utterly boring countdowns toward marks that everybody knows are going to be reached. . . . The problem is phony enthusiasm over a purely symbolic event that's as predictable as sunrise."[14]

On the other hand, most baseball analysts do consider Ryan's seven no-hitters and his 300-plus victories truly great feats. When he completed his seventh no-hitter in May, 1991, he had more no-hitters than all the rest of the starting pitchers on active major league rosters. In his career he also had lost a no-hitter in the ninth inning five times—all with one out.

Most important and impressive was his 300th victory in July, 1990. As described in Chapter 1, his 300th win made him one of the twenty winningest pitchers in major league history, and it silenced critics who had questioned Ryan's mediocre won-lost record throughout his career. Although 5,000 strikeouts and seven no-hitters were impressive milestones, reporters wrote that 300 victories was a truly great baseball feat. Fittingly, on the occasion of his 300th win, reporters quoted Ryan's former critics, including Jim Palmer and Bob Feller, as agreeing that Ryan was worthy of induction into the Hall of Fame.

Passing the Test of Time

There is no question that Ryan has stood the test of time. On opening day of 1993, Ryan began his twenty-seventh major league season, setting another major league record. At the age of forty-six during the 1993 season, he was the oldest active pitcher in baseball. In 1993 one report reminded readers that only nine men in the history of the game had pitched at age forty-six.[15] In 1991 at age forty-four, Ryan became the oldest pitcher to throw a no-hitter, breaking the record he set the year before when he pitched his sixth no-hitter at age forty-three. (The previous oldest was Cy Young at forty-one in 1908.) In 1989 at age forty-two, he became the oldest pitcher to win an All-Star game; the previous oldest was Mickey Lolich at thirty-one in 1971. All of these facts were vigorously reported by the media, and writers have argued that Ryan's strikeout and no-hitter records may never be broken and that we might not see another pitcher win a 300th game for many many years.[16]

Remarkably, Ryan was still a "power pitcher" in his mid-forties, throwing in the mid-90 miles-per-hour range. As Ryan himself said at a press conference before his 5,000th strikeout: "I never anticipated pitching this long. I probably have surpassed any expectation I had by ten years. When I got into the game, power pitchers in their early thirties were basically out of the game."

The media presented Ryan's longevity in the game as especially noteworthy because he had struggled with control problems early in his career. In the *Houston Post*, columnist Richard Reeves recalled Ryan's last day as a Met in 1971, when manager Gil Hodges "told Ryan that he was finished in New York if he couldn't complete this game." According to Reeves, "Ryan lasted only until the fourth inning that night . . . walking eight or nine men." Reeves told us that Ryan cried in the locker room after the game.[17] Ryan overcame his control problems, and he learned to throw a curve and, later, a change-up to complement his fastball. In fact, he cited the development of the change-up as a key reason for his continued success in the last years of his career. Despite Ryan's own view of the importance of his change-up, sportswriters continue to dwell on his ability to throw the fastball in his mid-forties.

Reporters also told us that Ryan overcame several injuries during his career, including a tendon problem in his elbow that threatened his career after the 1986 season. Ryan told reporters at the press conference the day before his 5,000th strikeout:

> I really thought that my career was probably over in '86. . . . Dr. Jobe [a noted physician associated with the L.A. Dodgers] . . . really felt that it was a complete tear and that it would take the reconstructive surgery known as Tommy John surgery. At 39, I didn't feel that as far as time was concerned, that I had enough time left to undergo something like that. So I took the position that I was going to let nature take its course and see what happened in the off-season, so I pitched with it that year. Around the 15th of December, it quit hurting and I haven't had a problem with it to this day.

The media have emphasized that Ryan passed the test of time through his lasting accomplishments and lengthy stay in the major leagues. As I suggested at the end of Chapter 1, the media have presented Ryan's career through the narrative of the *quest*: He began his odyssey innocently in rural Texas Little League; it progressed through big major league cities like New York and Los Angeles, where he struggled to overcome the adversity of wild pitching, injuries, and mediocre teams; and it returned him gloriously to his Texas home, where he proved himself a victorious hero worthy of the sacred Hall of Fame. The media have not only reported Ryan's lengthy career but have reconstructed that career in heroic terms.

Ryan as a Representation of Cultural Ideals
"Heroes," Klapp wrote, "state major themes of an ethos, the kinds of things people approve."[18] It is clear that most members of the media who have covered Ryan's life and career approve of Nolan Ryan and the values they believe he symbolizes. Through media coverage Ryan has become well-known, not only for his baseball records, but also for his commitment to the values at the core of American society.

Ryan has been depicted as a hard worker, reinforcing an American value expressed in the Protestant work ethic. When he enjoyed early success with the Angels, *Sports Illustrated* quoted former player and then coach John Roseboro: "There is not one pitcher in baseball today who is in better shape than Nolan Ryan. He knows what work is, and he works."[19] Ryan's work ethic is best exemplified by his legendary workouts, which have been described in numerous articles. "On off days during the season," described one writer in a *Parade Magazine* feature story, "he lifts 5,500 pounds of weights in a variety of routines and repetitions, does one hour and 40 minutes of sit-ups, lifts, sprints, football-tossing, swimming and exercise-bicycling, and he adds 45 minutes of baseball drills."[20]

By following this regimented workout, he became, according to one fitness expert quoted in *Newsweek*, "a totally conditioned person," a quality "that separates Nolan from most ballplayers." *Life* reported that because of his workout routine, Ryan "carries only 12 percent body fat versus 20 percent for normal men."[21] Ryan's commitment to his workout was described by a USA Today reporter as so dedicated that even after throwing his sixth no-hitter, "Ryan was riding the stationary bicycle in the middle of the Rangers' clubhouse" as "his teammates were either fastening their ties, drinking another beer, or driving back to the hotel."[22]

Reporters have traced Ryan's work ethic to his youth in Alvin, Texas, and to his father, Lynn Nolan Ryan, Sr. "My dad was a hard-working man," Ryan was quoted in one story. "He'd work all day at the Amoco oil company . . . and get up at one in the morning to deliver The Houston Post. My brother Bob and I worked with him. I rolled papers on that corner from the time I was in the second grade until I was 14 and old enough to drive and deliver them myself." Another story indicated that "Ryan, still in grade school, started buying day-old dairy calves for $2 or $3 each." In these stories, reporters glorified Ryan's lifelong commitment to hard work.[23]

Ryan has been presented as committed to family. "He is the one who has kept everything together," Ryan's wife Ruth said in a Sports Illustrated feature titled "Citizen Ryan." "It would be so easy for him to go off, to just say, 'You take care of the kids while I go do this business.' He never says that. He always tries to make us part of everything."[24]

When Ryan signed with the Texas Rangers in December, 1988, for less money than was offered by San Francisco and California, he told reporters that "this was a decision not just made by me." He explained: "I have teenage kids. We will be able to maintain our home in Alvin, and our kids can keep going to the schools they are in."[25] And his decision to come back to the Rangers for the 1990 season was said to have been based on the vote of family members. Ryan told another reporter that he teaches his children "to be honest, have integrity, and learn to be happy without money."[26] Given Ryan's financial worth, this is a type of happiness his children probably will never have to experience.

Ryan has been presented as humble—as a "regular guy." One story quoted an Alvin businessman who said that Nolan is "as down-to-earth as a man could possibly be." "He's just a great person," said one of his teammates. "He breaks all the walls down, lets you be his friend." One reporter offered this example to illustrate Ryan's humility: "Just hours after Ryan threw his last no-hitter in 1981, he was pushing a lawn mower across his front yard. 'What's all the commotion?' he says. 'It's only a game.' Another refreshing thought."[27]

Ryan has been presented as wholesome. After his fourth no-hitter, Ross Newhan of the Los Angeles Times wrote that "Ryan, who seldom drinks, turned down a glass [of champagne] and said he would celebrate by taking Ruth out for a quiet dinner." Years later veteran Dallas writer Sam Blair told us that American League president Dr. Bobby Brown lauded Ryan for being a spokesman against the use of chewing tobacco, especially by children. Brown, a heart specialist and former ballplayer who returned to baseball to head the American League, said, "This may be one of the most important things Nolan has ever done."[28] In a recent article about Ryan's endorsement of Hall of Fame pitcher Satchel Paige's rules for keeping young, *New York Times* writer Ira Berkow quoted Ryan as saying: "You want to keep relaxed. I tried to teach my kids that. They've been around the clubhouse since they were little bitty tykes. . . . They've seen players get into fights, they've heard cussing, they've seen managers go crazy. I told them: 'That's not how we act.'"[29]

Ryan has been presented as loyal. When Ryan refused to take a cut in pay after the 1988 season to re-sign with the Astros and instead became a free agent, Houston owner John McMullen questioned Ryan's "loyalty" in the papers. The Houston press was quick to respond. Columnist Mickey Herskowitz stated simply that "Ryan's loyalty isn't the issue." Kenny Hand wrote that "McMullan cried foul and pleaded to anyone who would listen that Ryan committed the unpardonable sin of disloyalty," but that "in truth, McMullen will be the disloyal one—to the ticket buying public—by letting an institution like Ryan leave." And Dale Robertson wrote, "Suffice it to say that owner John McMullen, a man of no vision and a Stalinesque grasp of public relations, did nothing in his penny-wise, pound-foolish low-balling of Ryan that should have surprised us." Ryan left Houston and signed with the Texas Rangers, a move that was mourned but supported by admiring Houston columnists.[30]

In 1990 when the Rangers exercised their option to keep Ryan for a bargain $1.4 million, sportswriters in Dallas commended Ryan's refusal to renegotiate as other athletes would. Ryan was quoted by Randy Galloway, saying "That signature on your contract is the same as your word."[31]

Finally, and perhaps most important, Ryan has been presented as an American cowboy. Stories have used the cowboy and the mythos of the West to show the values that Ryan symbolizes as values of our nation's past. In his thesis on the nineteenth-century frontier, Frederick Jackson Turner argued that "our national customs and character, indeed, our sources of success as a people, were largely a product of our frontier experience"— an experience that forms an integral part of the mythology of America. One observer described the cowboy, the central figure in the frontier thesis: "Daring, noble, ethical, romantic, he permeates our popular media to this day. He personifies our national self image."[32]

If the cowboy is one of the most heroic figures of our American heritage, then viewing Ryan as a cowboy who represents the core values of this heritage makes him a uniquely American hero. David Kaplan of the *Houston Post* quoted a Houston attorney who said that Ryan is "sort of like Gus [McCrae] in *Lonesome Dove*. He takes his hat off, wipes his brow, and gets back to what he's doing. 'Ah shucks, I pitched a no-hitter. It weren't nothing.'" Dallas sportswriter Skip Bayless, on the other hand, insisted that "Ryan is our very own Capt. Call of *Lonesome Dove*." In either case, Ryan is represented as a classic American hero.[33] And if the cowboy connection weren't enough to confirm his status as an American hero, another sportswriter informed us that Ryan "is related through his mother to John Hancock, one of the signers of the Declaration of Independence."[34]

Members of the media are not the only people who have exalted Ryan as a hero. Members of the franchises for which Ryan has played have lauded his commitment to these mainstream values. One part-time security guard, for example, remembered: "Even after his near no-hitters he was down in the weight room and on the exercise bike the next morning. That tells you something right there about what kind of guy he is."

The former Ranger president described Ryan's meaning to the franchise in broader terms: "Nolan's quiet, humble approach to the game and to his own stature in the game has meant more to this franchise than his presence on the mound. He's a tremendous role model, not just for kids, but for other players and for all of us. He will leave a lasting message about class and quality that is just incredible." As the Rangers treasurer concluded: "When you deal with many players who have been coddled their entire lives and who often seem to cultivate a certain arrogance, it is refreshing to see any player who is just a regular guy. And then to see Nolan Ryan, who by anybody's definition is a superstar, and he is still able to relate to fans and to you and me, it's just incredible."

It is not surprising that few people have been willing to go on the record with criticisms of an American hero. The only mildly negative comments members of the Ranger franchise were willing to make about Ryan—and they are only mildly negative—were that he is not effusively friendly and that he has cussed on the mound on certain occasions, as when television cameras caught him mouthing a version of the "F word" after a no-hit bid was broken up in the ninth. "Whatever his imperfections," wrote one reporter, "they are not public domain."[35]

Assessing Media Coverage of Ryan's Heroism

Although the test of time determined heroism in earlier days, the test of the media may be a more definitive and rigorous standard for contemporary heroism. Despite the misguided criticisms referring to the sports media as the "toy department," sports can be one of the most critical of all news departments. Sports reporters and editors do celebrate when the home team wins, but they are the quickest to turn, castigating players, coaches, and franchise executives when the home team loses. And given the modern mass media's incentive for publishing and broadcasting sensational, conflict-oriented scoops, sportswriters often publicize the private, off-the-field lives and problems of sports figures.

Surprisingly, Nolan Ryan has emerged from over twenty-five years of media coverage with very little negative press about his character on or off the field. I say this is surprising because reporters have the ability to dig up the smallest pieces of dirt about our professional athletes. For example, Skip Bayless, who earned a reputation for slashing the most revered sports figures (including Tom Landry whom he called "God's Coach"), wrote about his efforts to find a skeleton in Ryan's closet. The columnist informed readers about his checks with anonymous sportswriters about Ryan's background, assuming that "no wealthy baseball star can be as humble and clean-living as Ryan's supposed to be, and beat writers usually know every speck of dirt." The only thing Bayless discovered was that Ryan "was accused of scuffing the ball on his change-up in the National League." In the same column where Bayless critiqued the "baseless cockiness" of former Ranger manager Bobby Valentine, he concluded, "Nolan is Nolan—just an ol' cowpoke. And I don't mean that negatively. He's so respected in our industry because of the way he carries himself. He's as far from a prima donna as you can get."[36] A Dallas television critic who reviewed a video on Ryan's life titled "Feel the Heat," concurred, writing that "Mr. Ryan somehow has managed to remain smudge-free in an increasingly blotted game."[37]

Published tributes to Ryan's positive values have been easy to find. One *Sports Illustrated* feature put it this way: "In the tie-a-yellow-ribbon Americanism of the '90s, Nolan somehow has become the perfect oak tree. . . . Seen too much of the substance abusers and the night carousers and the uncoachable prima donnas? Here is a family man. Here is a businessman. Here is a cowboy."[38]

The conservative *Dallas Morning News* ran a rare sports editorial the day of Ryan's 5,000th strikeout, stating:

> Once there was no greater reason for the existence of professional athletes than to provide the young with heroes. . . . Unfortunately, in these times of pill poppers and gamblers, the private lives of too many ballplayers in all sports are hardly fit for prime time. A towering exception is Mr. Ryan. From work habits that have kept his middle-aged muscles fighting trim, to a clean-cut personal life straight out of the rural Texas he loves, Mr. Ryan is a hero for all ages.[39]

After his seventh no-hitter, in 1991, the *Morning News* ran another editorial about Ryan. "Nolan Ryan," it read, "is an obvious treasure for Texas sports fans hungry for heroes. But the message he delivers every time he steps on the mound is one that transcends baseballs, gloves, and bats. He is living proof that age and weary bones are no problem for someone who knows what he wants and is willing to work for it."[40]

Clearly, Ryan has passed the test of the mass media. However, in examining the media coverage of Ryan's career, from his days with the Mets as a wild rookie with potential to his days with the Rangers as the "ageless wonder" of 300 wins, it is clear that the media's test became biased over time. Though the media evaluated Ryan's status as prospect and his sta-tistics as a .500 pitcher in a relatively objective manner early in his career, they have celebrated his greatness in overtly subjective coverage in his later years. For example, Skip Bayless convinced us that all he could dig up about Ryan was that he scuffed the ball. But in his second autobiography, *Throwing Heat*, Ryan admitted that he once scuffed the ball and that he pitched "from about six inches in front of the rubber" when he "needed the big strikeout." Earlier in his career, reports also quoted Ryan admit-ting that he intentionally hit Red Sox batter Rick Miller with a fastball because he thought that Miller had been heckling him during the game. It appears that Bayless and the beat writers he consulted had not read—or remembered—Ryan's confession of these athletic improprieties.[41]

In another example, Mickey Herskowitz defended Ryan's loyalty in a 1988 column, asking the rhetorical question, "Has anyone ever heard him knock a manager, a teammate, an owner, anyone?"[42] Herskowitz's readers probably assumed not, but reports published early in Ryan's career sug-gest otherwise. After the Mets traded him to the Angels, the *Los Angeles Times* published Ryan's criticisms of his former manager, Gil Hodges, and pitching coach, Rube Walker. About Hodges, Ryan said, "To start with . . . Gil does not talk to anyone that much, and if you're a person having problems in his job like I was, you want a boss you can communicate with." About Walker, Ryan said, "As a catcher, he just wasn't able to help a pitcher with fundamentals. He wasn't able to pick up things while I was on the mound."[43]

According to *The Sporting News*, Ryan also criticized his teammates on at least one occasion when he pitched for the Angels. According to this report, Ryan criticized fellow pitcher Frank Tanana after Tanana claimed that his (Tanana's) arm was tired from overwork and that he was incapable of pitching 300 innings a season. Among the criticisms attributed to Ryan were the following: "I'm getting tired of people using me as an excuse"; "I'm being made to feel like the scapegoat for Frank's arm and I don't want it that way"; and "As far as I'm concerned, he [Tanana] hasn't worked hard or pushed himself since the All-Star break." The same article noted that Ryan "also took potshots at some of his younger teammates without nam-ing names" and it offered these quotes: "Too many young players pamper themselves and don't go all out"; "They don't have the obligation to the ball club they should have"; and "They're not giving an owner like Gene Autry a fair shake, especially for the money he has spent and for the faith he has put in people."[44]

Tracy Ringolsby revealed Ryan's uncharacteristic lashing back at Hall of Fame pitcher Bob Feller in response to Feller's unfair criticism about his preoccupation with strikeouts.[45]

Ryan's own loyalty to the game was questioned by managers Sparky Anderson and Billy Martin when Ryan refused to participate in the 1977

All-Star Game after he was selected to replace the injured Frank Tanana. At the time the normally low-key Anderson said that Ryan's decision not to play in the All-Star game was a "disgrace," adding that the game "is for the good of baseball and it helps the players' pension plan" and that "every player should be proud to be selected and to participate." The fiery Martin said that Ryan "should be suspended and not receive his salary for a week." Early the next year, after the Yankees' World Series victory ensured that Martin would again manage the American League All-Stars, he insisted: "I won't pick Ryan if he's won 40 games by the All-Star break. He can kiss my petunia."[46]

In the final analysis, Nolan Ryan is a sports hero because he has accomplished great feats, passed the test of time, represented positive cultural values, and passed the test of a sensation-seeking sports media. However, during Ryan's later years with the Rangers, members of the media have exaggerated Ryan's heroism and ignored earlier published criticisms of his less-than-heroic, but very human, traits.

Some reporters have gone so far in their enthusiasm for Ryan's heroism in recent years as to nearly deify Ryan. "Only on Sundays is Nolan Ryan not the most worshipped subject in [Alvin]," wrote John Strege for the *Orange County Register*, "unless his turn to deliver fire and brimstone at 95 MPH falls on the Sabbath. Is Nolan pitching today? Heaven can wait." Galloway's blasphemous tribute is further example: "God is Good. But Nolan Ryan may be better."[47] Fortunately, Ryan's own brother Bob was quoted in one story to qualify Ryan's sainthood: "'People hold him up as a perfect person,' Bob said. 'But I look at him with the criticalness of a brother. I feel like saying, 'Look guys, this is not Moses. He is not going to lead us into the Promised Land. He's got problems, too'."[48] Of course, Bob did not reveal Nolan's problems in the article.

A Hero for All Ages

If Nolan Ryan represents a "hero for all ages" as the *Dallas Morning News* editorial suggested, then he stands as a hero for the lost "golden age" of sports performance, as well as for the post-television age of sports consumption. In this chapter, I have focused on how the media presented Ryan as the lost hero of old and used him to reinforce traditional values of American society. In doing so, the media have performed what Benjamin Rader called a "compensatory function" by aiding the mass audience "in compensating for the passing of the traditional dream of success, the erosion of Victorian values, and the feelings of individual powerlessness."[49]

Fort Worth sportswriter Jim Reeves illustrated this compensatory function in his tribute to Ryan: "He represents all that is good and wholesome about the sport. He is a family man from Smalltown, U.S.A., an American legend who grew up on equal parts baseball, mom's apple pie, and smalltown values. He makes us all remember the sights and smells of our childhood. . . . Ryan reminds us of an era before substance abuse and rehab clinics, before labor strikes and lockouts."[50] The *Saturday Evening Post* put it even more directly, describing Nolan and Ruth Ryan as "almost too much to believe, a cliché coming true. They are what America, in its innocence, once believed of its heroes and hardly ever found to be true. And now, when we've become adjusted to the most cynical of athletes, we find the Ryans." And in Ryan's last year, in 1993, *Sports Illustrated* asked, "After Ryan retires at the close of this season, will baseball be left with any national heroes?"[51]

With these and similar published tributes, it is not surprising that Ryan has been touted as a possible political candidate. Although Ryan turned down the opportunity to run for Texas agriculture commissioner in 1990 and has told reporters that he is not interested in seeking public office, don't be surprised if Nolan Ryan is elected president of the United States in November of 2008 or 2012 — after a successful term or two as the governor of Texas.

On the other hand, media coverage also has presented Nolan Ryan as a contemporary hero who enjoys the benefits of our post-television, consumer age. "The hero-model moves with whatever is culturally significant at a given time," wrote Richard Lipsky, who argued that modern society is dominated by a "consumer ideology" such that "what is heroic, then, is what contributes to the common good of buying and selling."[52] Thus, Nolan Ryan is a modern-day hero not only because he has accomplished great feats or represented traditional values, but because he has cashed in on those feats to become a valuable commodity. The next chapter examines this aspect of the Nolan Ryan phenomenon.

Nolan Ryan, Inc.

"Nolan Ryan is one of the most desirable quantities in baseball."
—GEORGE STEINBRENNER, 1979

"I'm Nolan Ryan. If it's got to where you can't take TV sports because you're so sick of watching me sell things, then you need Nolie's sports mute."
—TANK MCNAMARA CARTOON, 1990

"Yeah, it's great to be appreciated. But somehow being able to still do with a baseball what I did twenty years ago has turned me into something else—an industry."
—NOLAN RYAN, 1992

4 While the media have presented Nolan Ryan as a genuine sports hero who reflects the cultural ideals of a previous mythical "golden age" of American sports, they have also shown him as a commodity and as a celebrity who reflects the capitalist values of American sports in today's consumer culture. As Ryan himself recognized in his most recent autobiography, *Miracle Man*, his success on the field and in the media have turned him into an "industry." In this chapter, I examine how the Nolan Ryan industry has been produced and promoted by his teams, by the media, and, ultimately, by his own actions and decisions.

Sports and American Business

To say that Nolan Ryan has been turned into an industry is to place Ryan and professional baseball in the context of American capitalism and modern consumer culture. Although the business of American baseball has been changed by television money and free agency, baseball has been a business enterprise since the formation of league play over a century ago. A player once said that "the great trouble with baseball today is that most players are in it for the money—not for the love of it, the excitement . . . and the glorious thrill of it all." The player was Ty Cobb, and he said these words in the "golden year" of 1925. As one observer put it simply, "Sports have *always* been based on commercial relations."[1]

Sports industries produce a variety of commodities that are sold or exchanged for profit in the marketplace. Each franchise sells tickets to fans who pay to see their team in a live sports event; the franchise also commodifies other things that are sold at the ballpark, including parking spaces, food and drink, programs, posters, team caps and clothing, and other products. Each league and each franchise sell the broadcast rights for live games to national and local media organizations. Those media organizations sell advertising time and space to companies that try to sell their products to the audiences.

Individual players are treated as commodities purchased by the different franchises though drafts, trades, or free agency. As sports industry analyst Paul Staudohar explained, players are valuable commodities for franchise owners, who enjoy unique tax advantages because "only sports businesses are allowed to depreciate their human assets."[2] The players also commodify themselves to increase their own earning power on the field through arbitration and free agency, as well as off the field through commercial endorsements, autobiographies and other books, and various investments.

Any examination of media coverage of a professional athlete is incomplete without recognizing that the relationship between sports and the mass media is defined by the business context in which it exists. Media critic Sut Jhally referred to this relationship as the "sports/media complex," and he summarized its importance to the analysis of individual athletes:

> The advertising revenues that manufacturers provide to media, who in turn buy broadcasting rights, are at the root of the sizable increases in player salaries over the last 30 years. The players then are able, like other workers, to sell their specialized labor power to employers for its market value. In addition to this, however, players are also trying to create a commodity that they can in turn sell—celebrity. . . . For many players, this may be of even greater value than higher sports salaries, in that they can trade in their celebrity for many years after they have finished playing.[3]

The media play a key role in producing and promoting players as commodities and celebrities through their coverage of sports. Without a doubt, the media have played a key role in creating Nolan Ryan as a commodity and as a celebrity and, in so doing, have reaffirmed the link between sports and capitalism in American culture.

Producing and Selling Nolan Ryan as a Commodity

The media have shown Nolan Ryan as an asset and a product to be exchanged or sold. Throughout his career, reporters have estimated Ryan's financial worth to his teams, to outside businesses, and to himself.

As discussed in Chapter 2, Ryan's financial impact on the teams for which he has played is virtually impossible to calculate precisely. Still, media reports have offered a variety of estimates of his monetary value to his teams. Some reports have quantified Ryan's direct effect on attendance. A few days before he was signed by the Rangers in December, 1988, the *Houston Post* examined Ryan's direct contribution to Astro attendance: in 1985 Ryan drew an average difference of 4,072 more fans per start; in 1986, a difference of 2,022 fans; in 1987 (when he and the team were in a slump), a surprising negative difference of −128 fans; and in 1988, a difference of 3,835 fans.[4] A *Dallas Morning News* story in July, 1991, reported that Ryan was directly responsible for an average of 4,633 more fans in his forty-nine starts at Arlington Stadium; another *Morning News* story in 1992 reported a similar figure for his eleven home starts that year.[5]

But these averages are misleading because attendance figures depend on many factors including the team's standings, the opponent, and the weather. Ryan also brought many other fans to the ballpark who purchased advance tickets hoping that Ryan would be in the rotation on that date. The Rangers' public relations director said he tells reporters that Ryan accounts for an estimated 8,000 more fans in attendance per start than other Ranger pitchers. In a telephone interview before the 1992 season, economist Gerald Scully said he estimates Ryan as indirectly responsible for bringing as many as 500,000 more fans to the ballpark each season.

Reporters have also emphasized the revenues Ryan has generated for baseball-related businesses inside and outside the ballpark. As described in Chapter 2, increased attendance has resulted in increased sales in concessions, souvenirs, and programs. Ryan has generated additional revenues for companies outside the ballpark as well, including hotels, restaurants, sports card shops, and retail sports outfits that carry Ryan paraphernalia—especially Nolan Ryan posters and Ranger shirts with the number 34. One report indicated that Ryan brought in as much as $1.7 million per year to the local economy.

When Ryan left Houston for the Rangers, one story projected that his move would affect the respective radio networks of the two franchises. The story quoted the director of the Rangers' flagship station WBAP as saying, "We will certainly be interested in exploring the possibility of coming into the Houston area so Ryan fans can listen to his games. . . . The Ryan deal has us thinking about going into new markets."[6] Ryan also was directly responsible for increasing the television ratings for ESPN's baseball coverage. In fact, the highest and third-highest rated baseball games on ESPN (through 1991) were Ryan's two attempts to win his 300th game. His unsuccessful attempt against the New York Yankees on July 25, 1990, received a 4.6 rating, while his successful attempt against the Milwaukee Brewers on July 31, 1990, received a 4.14 rating (each rating point corresponds to approximately 560,000 households).[7]

Nolan Ryan's Earning Power

Reporters have emphasized Ryan's earning power on and off the field. As in coverage of other high-profile athletes, sportswriters often have stressed Ryan's salary in stories, especially when he was negotiating or renegotiating with teams for new contracts. When Ryan became a free agent in 1979 after Angel general manager Buzzie Bavasi refused to renegotiate his contract *Sports Illustrated* quoted George Steinbrenner as saying, "Nolan Ryan is one of the most desirable quantities in baseball." A newspaper in upstate New York also quoted Steinbrenner saying, "You have to get the fans to the park somehow, and they come to see people hit home runs and strike people out."[8] When Ryan became baseball's first million-dollar free agent one month later by signing with the Astros, *Sport* magazine called him "not only the best-paid player in the history of baseball but one of the best paid players in the history of team sports." Ryan's attorney described the salary of $1 million per year as "truly historic."[9]

After the 1988 season, when Ryan's record was 12-11 with a 3.52 earned run average, Astro owner John McMullen asked Ryan to take a 20 percent cut in salary. The Houston sports media were quick to come to Ryan's defense. Kenny Hand wrote that McMullen's request was "the ultimate slap in the face to a Hall of Fame pitcher" and described the owner as being "disloyal" to fans. Mickey Herzkowitz supported Ryan by writing that he "has every right to test his value on the open market."[10]

In December, 1988, Ryan signed with the Texas Rangers for a reported $1.6 million in salary for the 1989 season (including a signing bonus and incentives that made the contract worth close to $2 million), with an option for the 1990 season worth $1.4 million. He later negotiated for a reported $3.3 million in 1991. In 1991 Ryan signed a new contract to play for the Rangers in 1992 and 1993 and offer "personal services" to the team for ten years after his retirement. One article reported the contract included a $300,000 signing bonus, $2.7 million salary for 1992, and $900,000 in deferred payments (at 8 percent interest). Ryan would receive a $300,000 bonus in July, 1992, as either a signing bonus or a buyout. To play in 1993, Ryan would be paid a $3.6 million base salary plus $1,000 for every inning pitched in 1992. He would also receive $210,000 annually during a ten-year personal services contract, which included personal appearance and the stipulation that he wear a Rangers hat when he enters the Hall of Fame.[11]

Throughout his career, sportswriters rarely challenged Ryan's salary figures; in fact, they often supported and even bragged about Ryan and his earning power on the field. Reporters have supported Ryan's salary demands in part because they have seen him as a humble, honest man who was not preoccupied with money, unlike many other athletes who are depicted as greedy and selfish. In 1976 Melvin Durslag wrote an article titled "Ryan Raps Pay Preoccupation" and quoted Ryan, then making $125,000, as saying that he had "never seen a ballplayer worth even

$250,000." The same article revealed that Ryan said, "A number of athletes make a fetish over salary and fringe deals not because they are personally obsessed with money, but because their vanity is at stake." It also reported that "Ryan said he abandoned hope of getting wealthy in sports."[12]

Years later when the Rangers exercised their option to keep Ryan for the 1990 season at an under-market value of $1.4 million, reporters commended Ryan's refusal to renegotiate as other athletes might have done. As Galloway quoted Ryan: "That signature on your contract is the same as your word." Two years later when Ryan, at age forty-five, was earning $2.7 million in salary and a total of $4.2 million for his entire contract, Galloway called him "the most underpaid player in baseball" and suggested that "Nolan, as always, let Rangers' management off easy."[13]

The media also supported Ryan's financial activities as an endorser and investor off the field. Early in his career, Ryan by choice did few commercial endorsements. Only after a few years of success with the Angels did he make his first endorsements: a print advertisement for Acme cowboy boots (which, somewhat ironically, ran in the March, 1976, issue of *Playboy*) and a television commercial for an airline with Franco Harris and Rick Barry. He also published his first autobiography, titled *The Other Game*, with Bill Libby.

At this early point in his career, however, Ryan constantly told reporters that he was not interested in making money off the field. "I'm away so much with the team," he told Pete Axthelm in 1975, "that I try to spend all my free time with my family. I could make more appearances and get more attention other ways, I guess, but this is the life I want. It's just a matter of taste." Melvin Durslag quoted Ryan on his lack of interest in off-the-field endorsements: "I have turned down a lot of business opportunities . . . and I rarely make speeches, even for pay. I do a few outside things, but I'm not bugged over money. I feel I have all I can do to keep my mind on conditioning and on pitching."[14]

How things change over time! In 1992 Ryan admitted in *Miracle Man* to being "more comfortable" with endorsements: "I have a better idea of what they want, and I'm learning to deliver with every take. . . . Since the extra income allows me to do things for my family I wouldn't have been able to do otherwise, I carefully select the right ones and accept them."[15]

The carefully selected "right ones" have included print, radio, or television ads for Advil, Bic shavers, BizMart office supplies, Duracell batteries, the *Fort Worth Star-Telegram*, Justin Boots, Nike, Southwest Airlines, Stadium Lincoln-Mercury, Starter Apparel, Whataburger, Wrangler Jeans, Kelloggs Corn Flakes, and others. As one advertising executive put it simply, "He's real well paid."[16] An April, 1992, issue of *Forbes* estimated that Ryan also made at least $1.8 million in 1991 from signing autographs alone, though others have insisted that he makes no money from autographs. Media stories have also told us about Ryan's investments, most notably his ranches of registered Beefmaster cattle and his two banks in Texas. According to Ryan's own public estimates, "I paid $600,000 for the Danbury bank and it has grown from assets of under $10 million to more than $24 million. The Alvin branch gives us about $20 million more in assets." Another report revealed that Ryan had merged the two banks, renaming them "Express Banks" and raising assets to $33 million.[17]

Predictably, reporters have glorified Ryan's performances as an endorser and investor as they have glorified his pitching performances on the mound and his life-style off the mound. In an article that appeared on the front page of the *Dallas Morning News*, the vice-president of a Fort Worth advertising agency said that Ryan is "such a good spokesman" because "he uses the products he talks about." An advertising executive from Houston who ran the Whataburger account said that "the primary reason Whataburger selected Mr. Ryan was because he is a family man."[18] A *Los Angeles Times* article on Ryan's endorsements quoted Ryan's agent Matt Merola, who offered this assessment of Ryan's appeal as an endorser: "He's the Jimmy Stewart of players. No one has higher credibility. He embodies everything everyone loves. . . . If you want someone you can believe in, Nolan is it."[19]

Surprisingly, though, Nolan Ryan was not listed among the forty highest paid athlete-endorsers in *Forbes* magazine for November 23, 1992. This is surprising because Cecil Fielder was ranked fortieth with total earnings of $4.6 million ($4.5 million in salary and $0.1 million in other income), and Ryan's 1992 income was reported to be $4.2 million; however, $900,000 of that $4.2 million was deferred. Even so, another article estimated that Ryan's 1992 earnings off the field were close to the $4 million figure, not counting his banks and his ranches.[20]

Media stories have also glorified Ryan as a smart and frugal businessman. "He still is one of those guys who travel the extra mile for gas at $1.06 per gallon if the local station is charging $1.10," wrote Leigh Montville in *Sports Illustrated*. "I'd use another word for him, 'tight,'" said Sonny Corley, president of the Danbury bank. "But that's all right, because I'm tight too."[21]

Ryan himself confirmed in *Miracle Man* that "no matter what my income has ever been, I've tried not to lose sight of the value of the dollar and what it takes to earn a living in the normal world." On the other hand, Ryan admitted losing millions of dollars in bad tax shelters, poor oil investments, a faulty thoroughbred horse breeding program, and other bad investments. But these disastrous financial decisions have received relatively little press coverage. In 1992, for example, Ryan was sued by the Northwestern National Insurance Co. of Milwaukee, which claimed that Ryan was late paying off a note. The story was merely summarized in a brief report in the business section of the *Dallas Morning News*.[22]

As the sports media juxtaposed Ryan's heroic values of hard work and modesty with his achievements and earning power on and off the field, it has reaffirmed his identity as a successful professional athlete and businessman. In so doing, the sports media have also promoted the business of baseball in American culture.

The Cost of Money in Sports
The media's overemphasis on the business of sports has far-reaching consequences, as all fans, young and old, have become preoccupied with the economics of virtually every aspect of sports. Writing for *Sports Illustrated,* Tom Verducci said that this overemphasis on the business of baseball means that "players are defined by how much they make, not by who they are and how they play."[23] In 1990 the worth of Nolan Ryan's rookie card received national attention when a clerk in an Illinois sports card shop sold one to a thirteen-year-old boy named Bryan Wrezesinski for $12.00 instead of $1200. The owner of the shop, a middle-aged man named Joe Irmen, asked the boy to return the card because of the mistake and offered him $100. But the boy, with the blessing of his father, refused the compensation and kept the card, resulting in a year-long courtroom drama between the two parties.

Reporters seasoned the story with discussions of ethics and honesty, especially when they discovered that Wrezesinski was not a naive little leaguer who didn't know any better, but rather a knowledgeable collector (of about forty thousand cards) who admitted under oath that he knew the card was worth $650–$900. "Somehow the picture of a fuzzy-cheeked adolescent became all that is wrong with baseball cards, an innocuous hobby turned hard-nosed $200-million-a-year business where people try mightily to take advantage of one another," wrote one reporter.[24] Eventually, the two parties agreed to auction the card off for a Chicago charity. The bidding stopped at $5,000.

I experienced a similar consequence of the media's business emphasis one night after a game at Arlington Stadium in 1989, when I watched a crowd of people gather at the clubhouse gates, seeking autographs. One ten-year-old boy stood with a couple of experienced autograph hounds and two rookies, all of whom were about the same age. The youngsters waited near a bus outside the gates that would take the players to the airport for a road trip. As they stood waiting for the players, the ten-year-old leader acted as a marketing consultant for the rookies, sharing his techniques. "The first thing you gotta do," he told the bright-eyed rookies, "is stand close to the bus. A lot of players will pretend they don't see you but then break down and sign one or two right before they get on." The rookies nodded, taking mental notes on their unsigned baseballs. "Then you have to stick the ball way over the rope here so they see it. And you have to talk loud, but you can't yell. Oh, and say, 'Mr. Witt, Mr. Fletcher.' If you yell out their first names, they don't usually sign them."

He asked the two rookies whose autographs they were seeking that night. One said, "Kevin Brown," to which the consultant nodded approvingly and said, "Oh, that should be cake. And if he has a good rookie year this year, it'll be worth a lot of money next year." The other boy answered proudly, "Ruben Sierra [former Ranger outfielder]." The consultant shook his head disparagingly. "You'll never get that one, I can tell you right now. Ruben hardly ever signs." He continued to shake his head but offered some feeble encouragement. "If you get it though, it'd be worth a lot of money. I could prob'ly sell Ruben's autograph tomorrow for at least twenty-five bucks." He paused, then advised, "Of course, if you get it, you better keep it 'cause you prob'ly won't get another one."

A middle-aged man standing among these kids sighed and said, "When I was a kid, we used to collect baseball cards and get autographs for the fun of it."

The ten-year-old entrepreneur looked up at the man and said, "Too bad."

Promoting Nolan Ryan as a Celebrity

As the relationship between the mass media and professional sports has flourished, so has the sports celebrity. Daniel Boorstin defined celebrities as "human pseudo-events" who are known for their "well-knownness"—for the press coverage and media attention they generate rather than for their accomplishments.[25]

According to some, Nolan Ryan has indeed become known as much for his coverage in the press as for his performances on the mound. Ryan did not get much playing time early in his career with the New York Mets, but because of his unique ability to throw the ball hard, he received much media attention. At that time Ryan suffered blisters on his fingers from the friction caused by throwing the ball so hard, a condition that garnered him additional media attention. Gus Mauch, the Mets' trainer, suggested that Ryan try pickle juice to toughen the skin. Suddenly, stories about Ryan's use of pickle juice filled newspapers and magazines. In a brief article titled "Brine for Nolan Ryan," *Life* magazine showed a picture of Ryan's fingers dunked in a jar of pickle juice and quoted him as saying: "I've never eaten a pickle . . . and I'll bet they taste as bad as they smell. I can even smell that brine out on the mound."[26]

A feature by Jack Lang in *The Sporting News*, titled "Pickle Juice Sweetens Life for Ryan," showed Ryan dipping his pitching fingers in a jar of pickle juice and Leo Polanski, manager of a Bronx delicatessen, pointing to a jar labeled "Mets pitching juice." Lang suggested that "whether or not he wins any other honors in his freshman year, Nolan Ryan is almost certain to be named 'Man of the Year' by the Pickle Packers of America." As the *New York Times* put it in retrospect years later, "Pickle brine. Nolan

Ryan didn't know what it was but he helped make it famous for a while" (and vice versa).[27]

A few years later, *Sports Illustrated* told us that Ryan had abandoned the pickle juice in favor of tincture of benzoin. When he joined the Angels, stories revealed that Ryan had a new approach to his blisters. As Ross Newhan quoted him: "What I do now before I pitch is take a scalpel and peel back the loose skin on the tip of the finger. I leave it almost raw and ready to bleed, but I haven't had any problem with blisters."[28] All this media attention to the fingers of someone who at this time (before the 1972 season) had compiled a major league record of 29-38.

Ryan also received press attention in his first year as an Angel for his use of another interesting substance: rattlesnake oil. Writing for *The Sporting News*, Dick Miller reported that Ryan gave a bottle of snake oil to fellow pitcher Clyde Wright, who had been suffering pain in his shoulder. According to the article, "Dr. Snake Oil" Ryan had discovered the "cure-all" the previous winter when he went hunting with an old man who used the oil to treat his crippling arthritis. "You gut him," Ryan said about the snake – not the arthritic man, "and boil the oil." He added, "You'd be surprised how much oil you get out of a three or four-year-old rattler."[29]

Ryan finally gained press attention for his accomplishments on the field when he began to succeed with the Angels. In 1973 he was 21-16 and registered a season strikeout record with 383; in 1974 he was 22-16 and threw two no-hitters. Because of the amount of publicity related to these on-the-field accomplishments, the Greater Los Angeles Press Club honored Ryan as one of five California "Newsmakers of 1974" at the group's thirteenth annual awards banquet. This signified that the media gave Ryan extensive media coverage, then gave him an award for receiving so much of their coverage, and then gave him additional coverage for accepting their award. The celebrity business perpetuates itself very well.

Success on the field continued for Ryan in 1975, as did media attention off the field. Ryan made a cameo appearance on a soap opera, appropriately titled *Ryan's Hope*. That same year there were preliminary discussions for a possible made-for-television head-to-head confrontation between Ryan and Japanese slugger Sadaharu Oh, for which Ryan would make $20,000 per strikeout and Oh would make $20,000 per home run. According to one article, "Ryan issued the challenge while his agents, Mattgo Enterprises of New York, were negotiating with network television officials. 'It's an outgrowth of this spring when he said he would like to bat against me,' said Ryan."[30] But this televised "pseudo-event" never came together.

Despite coverage of Ryan's exploits on and off the field, his press award, his endorsements for cowboy boots, and the publication of his first autobiography, sportswriter Dave Anderson insisted in 1978 that Nolan Ryan would not be a celebrity for long. Anderson predicted, inaccurately, that Ryan's status as celebrity would fade because of Ryan's low-key personality: "He's not the type for the gossip columns. He's too homespun, too quiet, too private. More than anything else, he's too uncomfortable with controversy."[31]

Anderson couldn't have been more wrong, as Ryan's celebrity status would reach incredible heights in his years with the Texas Rangers. With each of his milestone accomplishments, Ryan's status as hero and celebrity was reaffirmed. "If someone does a heroic deed in our time," wrote Boorstin, "all the machinery of public information—press, pulpit, radio, and television—soon transform him into a celebrity."[32]

Ryan's "machinery of public information" has taken many forms throughout his career, especially with the Texas Rangers. Ryan's life has been the subject of three published autobiographies: *The Other Game*, with Billy Libby, in 1977; *Throwing Heat*, with Harvey Frommer, in 1988 (with a revised paperback edition in 1990); and *Miracle Man*, with Jerry Jenkins, in 1992. He also co-authored *Nolan Ryan's Pitcher's Bible* in 1991 with Tom House, which offered a "how to" manual for "power, precision, and long-term performance," and *Kings of the Hill* in 1992 with Mickey Herskowitz, which presented Ryan's "irreverent look at the men on the mound."

Newspaper and magazines have run stories about virtually every aspect of Ryan's life on and off the field. "Instead of inventing heroic exploits for our heroes," Boorstin cautioned, "we invent commonplaces about them."[33] So there have been stories about Ryan's early childhood experiences, about his least favorite jobs in life, about his pre- and post-game routines, about his cattle ranching activities, about his hobbies of hunting and fishing, about his commercial endorsements, about his birthday celebrations, about his favorite color and his favorite type of music, and on and on. A paper published in Ryan's hometown of Alvin, Texas, offered a weekly section called "The Ryan Watch," which chronicled Ryan's activities.

Ryan has also been the focus of attention in other forms of popular media. He has been the subject of poems, two of which are featured in Gene Fowler's book *Center Field Grasses: Poems from Baseball*. He is the subject of a song written and performed by country-western singer Jerry Jeff Walker, "Nolan Ryan (He's a Hero to Us All)," on Walker's *Navajo Rug* album. He has been the subject of several videos, including a "video baseball card" titled "The Ryan Express" and a video of his career titled "Feel the Heat," which aired on PBS in 1992.

He has been the subject of several cartoons. A 1988 "In the Bleachers" cartoon showed a young boy holding his hand in pain as a mother yells out, "Underhand, Nolan! Throw the ball underhand!!" A 1991 "Shoe" cartoon showed Shoe as a despondent pitcher who has just struck out a hitter but tells his catcher that "at this rate, I'll have to pitch until I'm 340 years old to catch Nolan Ryan." And a 1990 "Tank McNamara" strip takes aim at Ryan's television commercials by featuring Ryan in a commercial pitching a new product: "I'm Nolan Ryan. If it's got to where you can't take TV sports because you're so sick of watching me sell things then you need Nolie's sports mute. Special electronic circuits recognize my voice patterns and then instantly cut off your TV's sound for the next 30 seconds. Because, hey, I might break another record, and if you think it's bad now. . . ." Several editorial cartoons in the *Houston Post* lampooned Ryan's anticipated 1990 candidacy for Texas agriculture commissioner.

There have been calls to build statues and to rename streets and parks in Ryan's honor, especially in Texas. In July, 1988, before Ryan left the Astros for the Rangers, Houston columnist Tom Kennedy made a public call—a request for $1 from every Ryan fan—to commission a life-size bronze statue of Ryan to be placed outside the Houston Astrodome. When Ryan departed later that year, the same columnist said that the Astro management's lack of interest in the statue had been evidence "they never intended to re-sign Ryan."[34]

In Ryan's hometown of Alvin, a statue was commissioned to be erected in front of city hall, not far from the Nolan Ryan Museum, which was approved by the Nolan Ryan Historical Foundation. In 1991 the Texas legislature approved the renaming of a section of Texas State Highway 288 near Alvin as the "Nolan Ryan Expressway" after some mild opposition from a few Democrat state senators.

Finally, Ryan has developed his status as celebrity through his commercial endorsements. "Endorsement advertising not only uses celebrities," Boorstin pointed out, "it helps make them." And Ryan realizes this, as he said, "I've become as well known for Bic shavers and Advil as for my pitching." (When I asked a group of students in one of my classes in California, "Who is Nolan Ryan?", one non-baseball-fan said tentatively, "Isn't he the guy on that Advil commercial?")[35]

As a celebrity, Ryan has not only endorsed corporate products, he has also endorsed candidates for political office. When he declined to run for Texas agriculture commissioner, he endorsed incumbent Jim Hightower's Republican opponent, Rick Perry. "It's time agriculture had one of its own to head the Texas Department of Agriculture," Ryan said in a radio ad that aired during commercial breaks on the Rangers radio network. "That's why I'm proud to support Rick Perry. I know you'll do the same." At a news conference in October, 1990, Ryan reaffirmed his support for Perry. Perry defeated Hightower the following month.

Ryan's endorsements of Republican candidates drew criticism from Democrat officials in Texas, particularly as efforts were being made to rename part of a state highway in his honor. "It could set a bad precedent if we start naming highways and buildings for politically active individuals," said Democrat state Senator John Whitmire.[36]

Ryan's endorsements of particular values, issues, and life-styles have also received public attention. When he published *Miracle Man*, for example,

Ryan offered his opinions about Magic Johnson (he has "a problem with making a hero out of him because he has AIDS"), Martina Navratilova (he does not agree with "her bisexuality" but agrees she made a good point when "she said that if a woman athlete had announced she had AIDS and that she had slept with a couple hundred men" that "she would be called a tramp"), Ted Kennedy (he says Kennedy "hasn't helped [his] attitude toward the Democrats"), the Gulf War (he thought it was justified but that "we should have gone ahead and finished it off"), marriage ("the divorce rate just shows how screwed up our society is"), and the criminal justice system ("sure, okay, protect the person's rights when he's been accused, but once he's been convicted what would be so wrong with depriving him of his rights?").

There is no doubt that Nolan Ryan is a genuine sports hero. But the heroes of today can never be like the heroes of yesterday. Today's heroes must, by definition, also be commodities and celebrities. When today's heroes perform great deeds, they inevitably receive too much press coverage and too many offers for commercial endorsements. A cartoon from the October 15, 1990, issue of the *New Yorker* summarizes this point eloquently. The cartoon shows a teacher facing a class as she praises one of her students by saying, "Very good Gary: 'A hero is a celebrity who did something real.'"

Nolan Ryan is a celebrity who did something real. Unfortunately, as the autobiographies, commercials, and stories about his off-the-field activities proliferate, the significance of the real accomplishments becomes diluted by media coverage of the mundane. As Norman Corwin suggested, when sports and sports stars become overexposed in the media, "they become trivial in the same way that too much of *anything* becomes surfeit and loses importance and value as a commodity."[37] It is a sad but fitting commentary on Ryan's career when he himself recognizes that he has become "as well known for Bic shavers and Advil as for [his] pitching." But this fame has had a cost. As Ryan has gained some status as a modern media celebrity, he has lost some of his stature as a genuine hero. And it suggests that to some people Ryan himself is no longer something real. He has become just another media creation, just another manipulated image.

The Image of Ryan and the Loss of Meaning

In the introduction of this book, I pointed out that most people do not know Nolan Ryan personally but rather through the media. And as the media have represented and reproduced Ryan as a commodity and as a celebrity, he has become a media image. The media image has several

characteristics that are important in understanding how audiences interpret their meaning in American society—and how audiences interpret the
meaning of Nolan Ryan.

First, the image is synthetic. It is an artificial creation, produced and
reproduced by the media. "Fact or fantasy," wrote Boorstin, "the image
becomes the thing" to the point that, "once the image is there, it com-
monly becomes the more important reality." Social critic Kenneth Gergen
concurred, writing that "so powerful are the media in their well-wrought
portrayals that their realities become more compelling than those furnished
by common experience." In view of this, he asserted, "it is to the media,
and not to sense perception, that we increasingly turn for definitions of
what is the case." In fact, Gergen concluded that the media have made
it virtually impossible to experience or identify with an "authentic self"
with real attributes and characteristics.[38]

As an artificial creation, the image is manufactured and manipulated
to serve a purpose. Ryan's image has been manufactured and manipulated
by major league franchises, interested companies, the mass media, and
Ryan himself to make money. Ryan's teams have used his image to increase
attendance. The Rangers placed a huge poster of Ryan above the entrance
to Arlington Stadium that could be seen from the nearby interstate—an
obvious promotion. Advertisers have used the Ryan image to sell products.
Ryan's status as cowboy has been used to sell cowboy boots and Wrangler
Jeans. As the caption to the Wrangler print advertisement puts it, "A Western
original wears a Western original." Ironically, as this advertisement has
been reproduced over and over, the Ryan image as well as the jeans are
no longer originals; they have become reproductions of originals. Ryan
also has learned to manipulate his image for profit. As he admitted in
his latest autobiography, he has become "more comfortable" doing commercials, and he is "learning to deliver with every take." But ironically,
as he sells his media image again and again for profit, he reduces the value
of his identity as a Hall of Fame pitcher.

Second, the image is distorted. As an artificial and manipulated creation, certain characteristics of the image are exaggerated while others are
suppressed. Boorstin suggested that creators of the image will "exclude
undesired and undesirable aspects" and exaggerate a few key aspects to
create a "vivid portrayal" of the image that is "simpler than the object it
represents" and does "not offend."[39] As the desirable features are exaggerated, the image becomes larger than life—larger than the life of the
person the image represents. In the process the varied and sometimes con-
flicting dimensions that make a person a unique individual are filtered
out to present a generalized caricature that will appeal to as many people
as possible.

Over the course of his career, the media have transformed Nolan
Ryan from a flawed mortal character to a heroic superhuman caricature—

the "ageless wonder." Although sportswriters revealed some of his com-
plexities and faults throughout his career, they glorified, exalted, and
even deified his persona in his later years. "Heroes, are for comic books
and dreams," said Mike Lopresti in *USA Today*. "But not always. Anyone heard anything bad about Nolan Ryan lately?" An ESPN announcer
exalted him simplistically, saying that Ryan "*is* John Wayne." In these and
other oversimplifications and exaggerations, Ryan is transformed into a
caricature.[40]

As the Ryan image grew, it overshadowed other aspects of Ryan's life
and other aspects of the teams for which he has played. For example, the
Ryan poster on the Arlington Stadium entrance announced symbolically,
"This is where Nolie plays," while ignoring the contributions of Ryan's
teammates. Former Ranger outfielder Ruben Sierra was openly critical of
the attention to the Ryan image, saying, "I'm a great player too. But everything's 'Nolan, Nolan' around here."[41] Ironically, Sierra was traded to
Oakland in 1992 with two other players for Jose Canseco, one of the few
players in baseball whose media image is as large as Nolan Ryan's.

Third, the image is fragmented. Although creators of the image tend
to exaggerate certain features to simplify its meaning, this meaning becomes disparate and diffused when the image is reproduced too often and
in too many forms. When this occurs, the image is not seen as a unified
portrait but as a collage of fragmented pictures, shifting constantly as
different people gaze from different angles. And the people who see these
different versions of the image interpret them and relate to them in different ways.

Despite the effort of the media in recent years to present him as the
hero of old, the Ryan image has been reproduced so many times and in
so many ways that audiences have been saturated. We've seen Ryan the
Hall of Fame power pitcher, Ryan the cowboy rancher, Ryan the family
man, Ryan the workaholic, Ryan the profit-seeking endorser, Ryan the
conservative Republican, Ryan the hunter and fisherman, and even Ryan
the sex symbol (an image I will discuss in the next chapter). To the extent
that audiences develop para-social relationships with celebrities, our relationships with Ryan's image become fragmented as we try to process these
varied images. "With the disappearance of the true self," said Gergen, "the
stage is set for the fractional relationship, a relationship built around a
limited aspect of one's being."[42]

Thus, it was much easier to admire Ryan when he was wearing a baseball uniform and throwing heat from the mound than when he wore a
business suit and pitched office supplies in a commercial for BizMart.

Finally, the image is public property. "An image is a visible public 'personality' as distinguished from an inward private 'character,'" wrote
Boorstin.[43] As a commodity, the image is a public product, and everyone
wants—and believes they are entitled to—a piece of the pie. For the celeb-

rity, the image is a public figure, and everyone wants—and believes they are entitled to—a picture or an autograph.

Though the media image is not the real person, the life of that real person becomes open to scrutiny by reporters and photographers and to harassment from fans and followers. For virtually all celebrities, the scrutiny and harassment are ongoing inconveniences of public life. "Every new town I arrive in means another crush of media and fans," Ryan said in *Miracle Man*. "Some people are so self-centered that all they're concerned about is what they want and not whether they're imposing on me or the rest of the fans who are being patient."[44] For some public figures, this scrutiny and harassment—and the potential danger from obsessed fans—are so overwhelming as to force restrictions on their lives. Ryan admitted some restrictions that have affected his family life: "There are times I'd like to take the kids out and don't. There are times I'd like to go to a Rockets game in Houston but don't. I can't even have a discussion over dinner in a restaurant without interruptions." Ryan also disclosed the fears of his wife, who worries about life in the future with Nolan Ryan the media image: "Ruth worries that I'll have an image like Jo DiMaggio, who still can't go out in public without being mobbed. That would be prison."[45]

As this suggests, the lives of the people close to the public figure also are affected. For example, when Ryan experienced some fame early in his career with the Angels, reports suggested that life was still normal for the low-key Ryans. One story quoted Ryan's assessment of the minimal cost of his celebrity status on his son Reid. "Reid," said Ryan, "is just like any other kid in the neighborhood. Nobody thinks of him as anyone special."[46] Fifteen years later, when the Ryan image covered the state of Texas, one headline summarized how things had changed for Reid: "Life Isn't Easy for Ryan's Son."[47] Reid pitched for the University of Texas during his freshman year in 1991, but he transferred to Texas Christian University for his sophomore year. "It's unbelievable the way people rag on him, the things people say," said Reid's coach at TCU in the article. Another recent story indicated that Ryan's wife and children are harassed constantly while out jogging or at school by friends, acquaintances, and even teachers who ask the family to get autographs for them. "The Ryans no longer allow people to drop things at the house [to be autographed] as if it were a Goodwill collection site," the reporter wrote.[48]

Members of the mass media are mostly responsible for the development of the Ryan image and for the resulting inconvenience and harassment that members of the Ryan family face. But Ryan himself must accept some responsibility for the overexposure of his image. He has agreed to grant interviews with so many print reporters and television announcers over the years. He has agreed to do not one, not two, but three autobiographies and several other books. And he has become "more comfortable" with doing print, radio, and television commercials. Unfortunately, as Nolan Ryan becomes more comfortable with his endorsements over the public airwaves, the private lives of the Ryans become less comfortable.

86

11. Ryan gets full-page coverage in the papers on the day of his 5,000th strikeout in 1989. Photo by Louis DeLuca, courtesy *Dallas Morning News*.

12. Ryan gets an entire special section in the Dallas paper following his 300th win in 1990. Photo by William Snyder, courtesy *Dallas Morning News*.

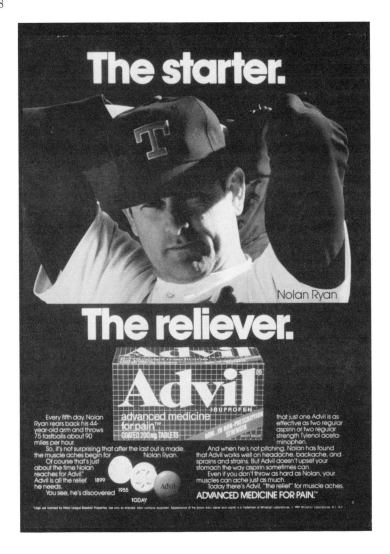

13. Ryan in a print advertisement for Advil. Courtesy Whitehall Laboratories.

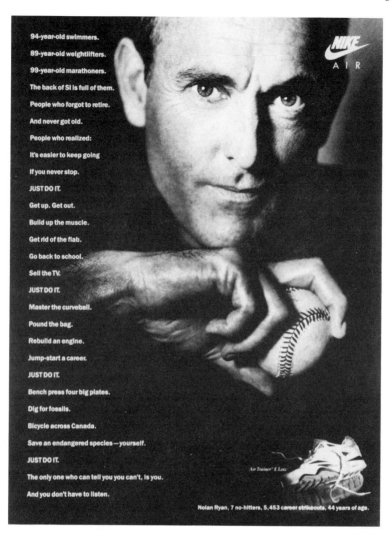

94-year-old swimmers.

89-year-old weightlifters.

99-year-old marathoners.

The back of SI is full of them.

People who forgot to retire.

And never got old.

People who realized:

It's easier to keep going

If you never stop.

JUST DO IT.

Get up. Get out.

Build up the muscle.

Get rid of the flab.

Go back to school.

Sell the TV.

JUST DO IT.

Master the curveball.

Pound the bag.

Rebuild an engine.

Jump-start a career.

JUST DO IT.

Bench press four big plates.

Dig for fossils.

Bicycle across Canada.

Save an endangered species—yourself.

JUST DO IT.

The only one who can tell you you can't, is you.

And you don't have to listen.

Air Trainer E Low

Nolan Ryan, 7 no-hitters, 5,453 career strikeouts, 44 years of age.

14. Ryan in a print advertisement for Nike. Courtesy Nike, Inc.

A Western original wears a Western original.

Cowboy Cut Jeans & Shirts

15. Ryan in a print advertisement for Wrangler. Courtesy Wrangler.

16. Rancher Ryan rides a cutting horse at Arlington Stadium in 1990. Photo by Linda Kaye.

17. Ryan wears baseballs in his holster in the Nike "Texas Ranger" poster. Photo by Bill Sumner, courtesy Nike, Inc.

18. For some fans at Arlington Stadium, Ryan *was* the Texas Rangers. Photo by Brad Newton.

19. Ryan signs autographs at the ballpark, a never-ending process for a baseball hero. Photo by Brad Newton.

20. Ryan throws out the "first pitch" at a ceremony to announce the building of a new stadium for the Rangers in 1990. Photo by Linda Kaye.

The Man on the Mound

"Ryan is tall, slender, deceptively strong, and certainly one of the handsomest men in sports."

—SPORTS ILLUSTRATED, 1974

"Nolan Ryan's arm is 35 inches long. It will fit perfectly in the Hall of Fame."

—ABC "WORLD NEWS TONIGHT," 1989

"300 wins and he still hasn't lost the crease in his jeans."

—AD FOR WRANGLER JEANS, 1990

Nothing in American culture has defined what it means to be a man more than sport. Brian Pronger wrote, "Sport in contemporary Western culture dramatizes myths; preeminent among them is the myth of masculinity." For the most part, the myth of masculinity reinforced by sport is a traditional one that emphasizes male strength, toughness, and competitiveness and implies the subordination of women and gay men. As sport sociologist Lois Bryson put it, sport "links maleness with highly valued and visible skills," and "it links maleness with the positively sanctioned use of aggression/force/violence."[1]

The role of sport in the promotion of a traditional sense of masculinity has been well documented. In his book *A Man's Place*, Joe Dubbert chronicled the link between sport and masculinity from 1880 to 1920 and examined the perpetuation of the view that sport built manly character, promoted order, justice, and physical fitness, and even prepared young men for war. "The record suggests that the rise of sport in America and its subsequent popularity after 1920 had much to do with preserving the masculine mystique," Dubbert concluded.[2]

As the "national pastime" of this early era, baseball was crucial in maintaining this "masculine mystique." Sociologist Michael Kimmel wrote that baseball helped to "reconstitute" masculinity during this period because it "maintained the 'rigid gender division and chauvinist masculine identity,' as well as the strict separation between whites and non-whites."[3]

Contemporary sports, especially as they have become more violent and

more commercialized, continue to play a role in reaffirming certain images of masculinity. Sociologist Michael Messner maintained that modern sports have become "one of the 'last bastions' of traditional male ideals
of success, of male power and superiority over—and separation from—the
perceived 'feminization' of society."[4] American football's hostile takeover
of the more pastoral baseball as our national pastime has reinforced a gro-
tesque form of masculinity that emphasizes sanctioned aggression, mili-
tarism, and the technology of violence.

The commercialization of virtually all sports has also provided more
opportunities for male participants than for females and has ultimately
marginalized women as cheerleaders, spectators, and advertising images.
Mark Naison's conclusion of twenty years ago still rings true today: "As
long as the social relations of contemporary capitalism generate a need
for violent outlets and a vicarious experience of mastery in American men,
the corporations will be glad to finance the sports industry and mold it
in their own image."[5]

The sports media have been a powerful tool with which dominant
groups in government, media, and corporations have tried to reinforce
traditional values and images. "Sports tend to be presented in the media,"
said critic John Hargreaves, "as symbolic representations of a particular
kind of social order, so that in effect they become modern morality plays,
serving to justify and uphold dominant values and ideas." Scholars in various fields have demonstrated how sports reaffirm such mainstream values
as teamwork, competition, individualism, nationalism, hard work, and
achievement.[6]

Media coverage of sports reinforces traditional masculinity in at least
three ways. It privileges the masculine over the feminine or homosexual
image by linking it to a sense of positive cultural values. It depicts the
masculine image as "natural" or conventional, while showing alternative
images as unconventional or deviant. And it personalizes traditional
masculinity by elevating its representatives to places of heroism and
denigrating strong females or homosexuals. In other words, the media reinforces the view of the masculine as the "norm" and anything else as "other."
For this to occur, according to R. W. Connell, masculinity must be embodied by an exalted hero or exemplar.[7]

Recent years, however, have witnessed some serious challenges, both
good and bad, to the dominance of traditional masculinity in sport. Women's
sports have risen at the collegiate and professional level, especially women's
golf and tennis. Gays and lesbians have been presented as public figures
in sports, including tennis star Martina Navratilova and former major
league umpire Dave Pallone. Black athletes have become increasingly willing to challenge the dominance of white males in sport, as exemplified
by the charges of racism levied against the sports establishment by football's Jim Brown and baseball's Hank Aaron. Counter-culture images are

increasingly prominent in sports, from former football star Joe Namath, who wore panty hose in an advertisement in the 1960s, to tennis idol Andre Agassi, who proclaimed unabashedly that "image is everything" in a commercial in the 1990s. Finally, we have witnessed the advent of millionaire athletes who seem to put loyalty to self above loyalty to team, community, or anything else. Quite simply, the so-called "golden years" of sports—when our sports heroes were white, working-class, good-looking, high-scoring males—have been gone for some time, much to the dismay of many white, middle-aged sportswriters.[8]

Given these challenges to the sports establishment and the tendency of modern sportswriters to write about the off-the-field lives of contemporary athletes, it is not surprising that the sports media have exalted Nolan Ryan as a genuine sports hero and have presented him as an ideal image of American masculinity. In Nolan Ryan, the media have rediscovered the lost sports hero of old. And in covering this lost hero, reporters and sportscasters have reinforced a traditional image of masculinity, presenting him as the embodiment of male athletic power, as a family patriarch, as a white rural cowboy, and as a sex symbol.

Pitching with Power:
Ryan as the Embodiment of Male Athleticism

Scholars who study gender contend that male dominance is represented by the power of the male body. Connell wrote that traditional masculinity is seen in terms of the force and competence of the male body—terms that "define men as holders of power [and] women as subordinate."[9] The male body has come to symbolize power, and power itself is masculinized as strength, force, control, toughness, and domination.

Media coverage of Nolan Ryan has emphasized the power of the male body. Ryan has been called a "power pitcher" throughout his career. As reviewed in Chapter 1, early media coverage of Ryan's tenure with the New York Mets focused on the impressive but uncontrolled ability of the young Texan to throw the ball with amazing force. When he enjoyed success with the California Angels, his status as power pitcher was embellished by the sports media. One feature reported that a group of scientists timed two of his pitches at speeds of 100.8 and 100.9 MPH, the fastest pitches ever recorded. Coverage during Ryan's later years with the Astros and the Rangers marveled that Ryan, in his late thirties and mid-forties, still was a power pitcher who could throw the ball in the 90 MPH range. *Gentlemen's Quarterly* put it this way: Ryan "is grateful he can remain true to his singular purpose, which is to rear back, show his numbers and throw a baseball."[10]

The media have lauded not only Ryan's pure power, but also his use of power to dominate others. Reporters have celebrated Ryan's major league records of athletic dominance, especially his seven no-hitters and his 5,000-plus strikeouts. The no-hitter is one of the ultimate accomplishments of dominance over an opponent, and each of Ryan's was celebrated in media accounts. With each one, his previous no-hitters grew in significance. Writing for the *New York Times*, Dave Anderson retold the story of Ryan's second no-hitter on the occasion of his fourth one: "With two outs in the ninth, Norm Cash of the Detroit Tigers strolled up to the plate in surrender. Instead of a bat, he was carrying a broken-off piano leg. He even got into the batter's box with it before glancing back at Ron Luciano, the umpire."[11] Through coverage of Ryan's no-hitters and his milestone strikeouts, the sports media have depicted complete physical dominance over opponents as ultimate success.

Reporters mythologized Ryan's use of power even when he inadvertently injured others with it. A feature in the *Saturday Evening Post* titled "Nolan Ryan: Whoosh!" made a direct case: "All the while he was leaving a trail of incidents that formed a legend—or myth. The day he tried out with the Mets before signing, his fastball broke through the hands of catcher John Stephenson and broke his collarbone. At Williamsport, Pennsylvania, he bounced a warm-up pitch in front of the plate and gave catcher Duffy Dyer a concussion. Not with a fastball, but with a changeup."[12] Ryan's use of power—manifested in the total domination of others and the ability to hurt people—became baseball mythology.

Sportswriters also suggested that Ryan has displayed a "power personality" on the mound. "He lets you know that he's the man," said a backup catcher who spent time with Ryan in 1991. "You know that when he takes the mound, he's going to get it done." Houston columnist Kenny Hand described it this way: "His schtick is to grab a baseball, glare at the enemy, rock his hips gently, wind up and unleash a white blur. *Step right up, man-to-man, legend-to-legend, take your best shot* (emphasis is in original)."[13]

In his second autobiography, Ryan admitted that he is a different person when he takes the playing field. "When I'm out there on the mound," he revealed, "I don't consider myself a very nice person. I almost hate the players I'm pitching against. . . . Normally, I'm a very quiet and reserved person with a peaceful outlook on things. But when I'm pitching, I'm anything but that."[14] As noted in Chapter 3, Ryan even admitted that he intentionally hit Red Sox batter Rick Miller with a fastball because he thought that Miller had been heckling him.

Ryan's personality on the mound has been criticized by some of the players who hit against him. Ryan is "the best-liked, most-revered player in the game," wrote Tim Kurkjian in *Sports Illustrated*, "but he has a reputation among hitters for brushing back anyone he thinks has shown him up." Kurkjian quoted former Royals second baseman Terry Shumpert as being the most critical: Ryan is "the kind of guy who, if you get a good swing off him or you do something he doesn't like, wants to throw at you. . . . It puts you in a position where you don't know what to do. He's Nolan Ryan. Do you know of anybody who ever charged the mound on him?"[15] In 1993 Robin Ventura charged Ryan and got six "noogies."

Shumpert's criticism was supported by an incident involving Oakland Athletics outfielder Willie Wilson in a game in the 1992 season. Ryan was ejected—for the first time in his career—by plate umpire Richie Garcia, who said that Ryan intentionally hit Wilson in the thigh in the eighth inning. In his previous at-bat, Wilson had taken a big swing against Ryan before hitting a triple to right-center field. The practice of taking a big swing against a major league pitcher is one most pitchers resent, and Ryan reportedly shouted "an expletive" to Wilson after the swing. When Wilson entered the batter's box the next time, Ryan hit him with a fastball after throwing two pitches away. In the next day's sports pages, Wilson was openly critical of Ryan. The wire story in the *New York Times* indicated that "Wilson accused Ryan of arrogance," and quoted Wilson as saying, "He stares people down, he walks around on the mound, he just tries to intimidate everybody. This is his country, his town, his stadium. He's not a legend in my mind."[16] In the Dallas papers, Wilson was quoted as saying, "I lost respect for him for doing that. I don't think he cares about whether anybody has stature or not. Me and Nolan are two different things. I'm a guy who's gone to jail, I'm the bad guy, the eight-ball. He's the legend."[17]

Ryan's "power personality" also is exemplified by his ability to play with pain. One feature in *Sports Illustrated* quoted Ryan's teammate Phil Garner, who told of the arm pain that Ryan quietly suffered as a Houston Astro: "The casual observer would never know Nolan is hurting. . . . He never complains, never makes excuses. Everywhere else you hear about people with sore arms, sore backs, sore knees. The clubhouses are full of them. But you'll never hear any of that from Nolan Ryan."[18] A more recent article in the *Dallas Morning News*, titled "Pitching with pain not new to Ryan" told readers that Ryan had pitched his sixth no-hitter with a stress fracture in his back, but that because of his "will power," he was able to "block it out."[19]

Sportswriters presented these injuries as natural obstacles that Ryan overcame through his toughness as a successful male athlete. A feature in *Sport* magazine even recalled his toughness as a child: "'I remember when we first came to Alvin, this young wife, a friend of ours, kept pestering me to take Nolan to the doctor,' says his mother, 'because he didn't cry enough'."[20]

Although Ryan was eventually portrayed as a complete pitcher, writers continued to single out—even disembody—his power throughout his career. When he was traded to the California Angels in 1971, Angel general manager Harry Dalton was quoted as saying that the team had "obtained the best arm in the National League and one of the best in baseball." Later features in *Life* and *Gentlemen's Quarterly* presented photographs of Ryan's right arm; in the latter, past Dodger pitcher Don Sutton described Ryan's arm as "a howitzer." Correspondent Dick Schaap concluded his ABC "World News Tonight" report about Ryan's 5,000th strikeout by saying: "Nolan Ryan's arm is 35 inches long. It will fit perfectly in the Hall of Fame." An article in the *New York Post* noted that Ryan was "blessed with the most remarkable arm in the history of the game," and it cut off his legs as well: "Ryan has a pair of treetrunk legs that supply a great deal of the power behind his fastball." Even in the end, the force – the essence – of Ryan's power remained disembodied.[21]

Father Throws Best: Ryan as Family Patriarch

Social critic Gerda Lerner defined patriarchy as "the manifestation and institutionalization of male dominance over women and children in the family and the extension of male dominance over women in society in general."[22] This dominance is reinforced in gender-based divisions of labor when men are cast as the "breadwinners," "strong fathers," and "family protectors" while women are cast as "housewives," "nurturing mothers," and "sexual objects."

Gender roles have changed since the women's movement of the 1960s and 1970s, but many critics argue that America remains a patriarchal society. One sociologist argued, "There is no question that the father-breadwinner model established in the nineteenth and early twentieth centuries remains culturally dominant today, both in fathers' actual behavior and its media representation." Another author went so far as to say that representations of the modern-day father have remained patriarchical in the sense that "the contemporary revalorization of fatherhood has enabled many men to have the best of both worlds" because "they are more involved in what was once the exclusive domain of women but, especially in relation to children, they are sharing its pleasures more than its pains."[23]

The sports media play an important role in reinforcing the traditional masculinity associated with patriarchy. "The effect of sports," wrote sociologist Bruce Kidd, "is also to perpetuate partriarchy by reinforcing the sexual division of labor. . . . By publicly celebrating the dramatic achievements of the best males, while marginalizing females as cheerleaders and spectators, they validate the male claim to the most important positions in society."[24]

Media representations of Nolan Ryan have reinforced several features of masculinity associated with patriarchy. First, the media have reaffirmed traditional male-female relations in the family in its description of the relationship between, and respective roles of, Nolan and Ruth Ryan. Predictably, the media have presented Nolan as the breadwinner. One story in the *Saturday Evening Post* told of the struggles of Nolan early in his career to support the family: "The first year they were married [in 1967], Nolan made $1,200 a month for six months and worked in an air-conditioning shop the other six." When money was not a problem for Nolan later in his career, the media told us that he turned down more money from other teams to play with the Rangers so that, as Ryan was quoted in one story, "we will be able to maintain our home in Alvin, and our kids can keep going to the schools they are in."[25]

Ryan also has been portrayed as the protecting husband. Jack Lang of the *New York Daily News* even said that the trade that sent Ryan to California was motivated by the "fact" that "Ryan personally requested a trade because—says a Mets insider—he feared for the safety of his lovely wife in New York."[26]

In contrast, reporters have presented Ruth Ryan as the "woman behind the man." Reporters wrote that Ruth did not develop her own career interests; one article in the *Dallas Morning News* quoted her own admission that "I tried to go to college. I tried to keep up with my tennis and my ballet at first. . . . Some of the other wives I knew in baseball tried, but it just didn't work."[27] She has also been objectified as the "beautiful wife." One sportswriter for *Sports Illustrated* tackily put it: "By the way, think Nancy Seaver [Tom Seaver's wife] is cute? Get a look at Ruth Ryan sometime. A full 10 points."[28]

Reporters also told us that Ruth helped Nolan when he struggled in his career. Writing for the *New York Times*, Peter Alfano said that "Ryan was ready to retire" after his failure with the Mets but that "it was his wife, Ruth, who talked him out of it." Sportswriter Dick Miller told us that Ruth actually caught for Nolan in the off-season. "I've been working out with a high school catcher," Ryan said. "When he doesn't show up, I play catch with Ruth. She's throwing harder than I am."[29]

Reporters even told us that Ruth derived fulfillment from Nolan's pitching. Mickey Herskowitz suggested that Ruth would in fact be lost without Nolan's baseball: "'At times I get really tired of the hectic pace,' Ruth admits. 'Then I think about how much I would miss it, if he retired, and what I would do when spring training rolls around.'"[30]

In these ways, the media have reaffirmed gender-based divisions of labor in the traditional American family through Nolan and Ruth Ryan, and they have portrayed this division of labor as natural in presenting Nolan and Ruth as an ideal couple. "After 23 years, the man is still married to his high school sweetheart," confirmed Leigh Montville in *Sports Illustrated.* "The idea of staying married never came to debate," Montville continued. "Why not? Isn't that what you're supposed to do? The idea of raising a family was ingrained. Wasn't that what our parents did?"[31]

Second, the media have endorsed family patriarchy in glorifying Nolan's role as actual and symbolic father. Reporters have emphasized Ryan's relationships with his two sons, but not his relationship with his daughter. Dallas station KTVT's live television coverage of Ryan's sixth no-hitter focused in as younger son Reese, in a little Ranger uniform, sat next to Nolan in the dugout, rubbing his dad's back, which, as later was reported, had suffered a stress fracture.

During the 1991 pre-season, Ryan pitched against older son, Reid, who was then a freshman at the University of Texas, in an exhibition game. An article in the sports pages of the *Austin American-Statesman*, subtitled "Father Throws Best," noted that "mom Ruth threw out the ceremonial first pitch, her 'nervous fastball.'" Another article, on the *front* page of the same paper, deified father Nolan's relationship with his son: "The serious baseball crowd sat huddled against an intermittent evening breeze, watching father and son, concentrating, straining to see if they could detect the signs of greatness passing from the right hand of the father to that of his son."[32] (The Rangers won the game 12-5. Nolan pitched five innings and gave up three runs, all earned. Reid pitched two innings, giving up four runs, all earned.)

Ryan also has been represented as the symbolic father. "Ryan is providing stability and quiet leadership" to the "young, home-produced talent" of the Angels, wrote Axthelm in *Newsweek*. Years later, a report in *Time* extended the father metaphor more specifically: "His second family is the Ranger teammates, who mobbed him after the [sixth] no-hitter. Because some of them were barely in Pampers when Ryan first pitched for the Mets in 1966, the scene also suggested a Father's Day celebration—a bunch of baseball's children swarming around the grandest old man in the game." *Sports Illustrated* revealed that former Astro teammate Harry Spilman "is one of 10 current or former teammates who have named a son after Nolan." On Father's Day, June 16, 1991, ESPN's "SportsCenter" aired a report offering video proof of these little Ryans. Thus, the media have represented Nolan Ryan as the archetypal husband and father and, in so doing, have reaffirmed patriarchal values in American culture.[33]

Castrating Steers in the Off-Season: Ryan as Baseball Cowboy

Ryan's depiction as a rural Texas cowboy has also been used to define him not only as a uniquely American hero and a uniquely American commodity, but also as a uniquely American image of masculinity. "Nowhere is the dynamic of American masculinity more manifest," wrote Michael Kimmel, "than in our singular contribution to the world's storehouse of cultural heroes: the cowboy. It was the United States that gave the world the cowboy legend, and Americans continue to see him as the embodiment of the American spirit."[34] As reconstructed in media accounts of the West, the cowboy also is a white male with working-class values.

Throughout his career, Nolan Ryan has been portrayed as such a cowboy. The media have reported that Ryan and his wife grew up and still live in rural Alvin, Texas. They have told us that Ryan listens to country-western music, that his personal transportation is a pickup, and that his hero is John Wayne. The night Ryan pitched his seventh no-hitter, an ESPN sportscaster said of Ryan: "He's John Wayne." Of course, as a *Sports Illustrated* feature quoted Ryan's longtime friend and business partner, "in Texas he is bigger than John Wayne right now."[35]

Advertisers also have cashed in on the Western motif. One advertisement for Wrangler Jeans pictured Ryan on the mound, holding a baseball and wearing a glove, but sporting a cowboy hat and Wrangler Jeans. The caption to the ad reads, "A Western original wears a Western original." Although jeans may symbolize a number of values not inherent to the mythic West, media critic John Fiske has written that "the association of jeans with the cowboy and the mythology of the Western is still strong" for some people who see jeans as representing "freedom, naturalness, toughness, . . . hard work, . . . and, above all, Americanness."[36]

But Ryan is not merely a metaphorical cowboy for stories and advertising. "Ryan is no gentleman rancher," wrote Ron Fimrite in an article accompanied by several pictures of Ryan riding horseback on his ranch. "In the off-season, he's on horseback, riding herd, 'getting kicked, stomped, and hooked.'" Ryan's ranch manager gave more impressive testimony in another feature, again accompanied by photos of Ryan in action: "He helps us castrate the steers, dehorn 'em, everything. Nothing fazes him. I'll see him reach into the chute with that million dollar right arm and I'll say to myself, 'Are you sure you want to do that?' But he'll never buckle." In these images and characterizations, Ryan has been cast as the strong, tough, macho cowboy of our frontier past.[37]

Ryan has also been presented as a modern-day outdoorsman. In an article about Ryan's free agency after the 1979 season, "It's Fishing Season for Nolan Ryan," *Sports Illustrated* showed a picture of Ryan, dressed in a cowboy shirt and jeans, putting bait on the lure of a fishing pole. The caption revealed that Ryan was "doing a little fishing on his Texas ranch." Another feature, reprinted in "The Great Outdoors" section of the *Sacramento Bee* and titled "Nolan Ryan on the Hunt," showed Ryan in hunting fatigues. Ryan said, "As a youngster, when I wasn't playing some type of sport, I spent all my time out hunting." The reporter described the hunt: "Baseball's all-time strikeout leader watches intently for a trophy deer that lives in this canyon while telling about the whitetail buck he shot last year on his ranch."[38]

Reporters have used Ryan's status as cowboy and modern-day outdoorsman to display his ruggedness and toughness, as well as his commitment to the mainstream values of rural America. Representations of Ryan's work ethic, humility, wholesomeness, and loyalty were described in Chapter 3. "As we say in Texas," commented his high school principal in *USA Today*, "he is as common as dirt."[39] Through Nolan Ryan, reporters have reinforced an image of the American heroic male as one who embodies the frontier values of our country's past.

Not surprisingly, the cowboy of our past and the outdoorsman of the present usually are presented as white males. Attention was drawn to Ryan's identity as a white male athlete indirectly in coverage of his seventh no-hitter. Earlier that day, Rickie Henderson of the Oakland Athletics broke Lou Brock's record for career stolen bases. Henderson, who epitomizes the "cool pose" of the inner-city black athlete[40] with his brash, display-oriented demeanor, pumped his fists above his head and, as play was interrupted, told the crowd over a microphone: "Lou Brock was a symbol of great base stealing. But today, I am the greatest of all time." Later that same night, Ryan pitched his seventh no-hitter, then told reporters, "This no-hitter is the most rewarding because it was in front of these hometown fans who have supported me since I have been here. This one was for them."

In the days following these two milestones, sportswriters—most of whom are middle-class, white men—contrasted how the two star athletes handled the achievements. The *Sporting News* critiqued them in an editorial titled "A Day When Crass Gave Way to Class." "Too bad Henderson couldn't have handled his moment of renown with similar decorum," read the editorial. "It was a day when Henderson and Ryan displayed two forms of speed, but only one man exhibited class." Although the ethnicity of the two athletes was never mentioned, the media implicitly reaffirmed the masculinity embodied by Ryan's white, rural, mainstream values as preferable to the counter-culture masculinity represented by the "cool pose" of the black, inner-city athlete. Simply stated, when white reporters exalt white athletes and denigrate black athletes, they reinforce a racially based sense of masculinity whether they intend to or not.[41]

Manipulating an Image: Ryan as Sex Symbol

Traditional sexuality in American culture can be understood in terms of what Gayle Rubin has called the "sex hierarchy." The type of sexuality at the top of this hierarchy—"sexuality that is 'good,' 'normal,' and 'natural'"—is defined as "heterosexual, marital, monogamous, reproductive, and non-commercial." The view of traditional male sexuality dominant in American culture, as Gregory Herek argued, "requires not being compliant, dependent, or submissive; not being effeminate (a 'sissy') in physical appearance or mannerisms; not having relationships with men that are sexual or overly intimate; and not failing in sexual relationships with women."[42]

The symbolism of male sexuality has received much attention from scholars and popular writers alike. "The first thing to say about the symbolism of male sexuality," wrote Richard Dyer, "is that it is overwhelmingly centered on the genitals, especially the penis." Dyer wrote that the penis is "the symbol of male potency, the magic and mystery of the phallus, the endowment that appears to legitimate male power."[43] Of course, as psychiatrist Thorkil Vanggaard reminded us, there is a big difference between "penis," the organ, and "phallus," the symbol: "By the symbolic term phallus, we express the idea that beyond the practical function of the genital in its fully erect shape as a means of procreation and pleasure, it is a pictorial representation of the essence of manliness." Or as media critic John Fiske put it, "The phallus is a cultural construct; it bears a culture's meanings of masculinity and attempts to naturalize them by locating them in the physical sign of maleness—the penis."[44] Lynne Segal wrote, "Sport provides the commonest contemporary source of male imagery" because "the acceptable male image suggests—in its body's pose, its clothes and general paraphernalia—muscles, hardness, action."[45]

In particular, the media have used images of Nolan Ryan to reinforce a traditional image of masculinity and male sexuality. Throughout Ryan's career, sports reporters have commented on his physical attractiveness. He was described by sportswriter Ron Fimrite of *Sports Illustrated* in this way in 1974: "tall, slender, deceptively strong, and certainly one of the handsomest men in sports—a natural born hero." One year later, Fimrite was even more specific: "Ryan wears his hair short and neatly trimmed and is a tidy, unflashy dresser, unlike the many peacocks in modern sports. He is an uncommonly handsome young man with near-perfect features and a long, lean physique. With his good looks, lanky build and Texas drawl, he would seem a natural for Western roles in Hollywood." Ten years later, the same writer included Ryan's high school picture in a feature with the caption "Most Handsome Senior." In these descriptions and images, this white, middle-aged sportswriter directly endorsed an image of traditional male sexuality, contrasting it with nontraditional images of male sexuality embodied by flashier sports "peacocks."[46]

Frank Luksa, a white, middle-aged sportswriter in Dallas, described in detail Ryan's "everyman appearance" at the press conference before his 5,000th strikeout: "He wore a short-sleeved yellow shirt, with only the top button undone. Olive-green khaki pants. Brown stretch belt. Tan crepe sole shoes. He looked like anybody instead of somebody. What he didn't wear was a gold neck chain, neon bracelet, or earring. Nor a gaudy watch. Not even a pony tail, curls or bangs. No diamonds or insignia of his wealth and fame."[47]

Dave Anderson, another white, middle-aged sportswriter, when he described Ryan's unnoticed appearance at a restaurant early in his career with the Angels, wrote a telling comment: "'Table for Ryan,' he told the hostess. 'Oh, yes, Mr. Ryan,' the hostess, a young brunette, replied with hardly a glance at the man who is surely one of the most handsome in baseball. 'Right this way, please.' The waitress, a young blonde, did not seem to recognize him either. Neither did anybody at the other tables, not even any of the dozen teenage girls enjoying a birthday party."[48] Anderson presented a preferred image of male sexuality and, in doing so, revealed unwittingly that the preference was for his own white, middle-aged image. Ryan's physical attractiveness was apparently noted only by Anderson — not by the young women or the teenage girls.

It is rather unusual for male sportswriters to comment directly on the physical attractiveness of male athletes, though they all too often comment on the attractiveness of female athletes. However, in his representation as a wholesome, monogamous, heterosexual, white man, Nolan Ryan is an acceptable sexual image whose physical attractiveness can be described directly by white male reporters who tend not to write about the attractiveness of black or gay athletes or other alternative masculine images.[49] In this way, Nolan Ryan is a "safe sex symbol."

In an era of social and sexual consciousness about the AIDS virus, Ryan's emergence as a safe sex symbol seems appropriate for the times. It is not surprising, then, that Ryan commented on the Magic Johnson case in *Miracle Man*. "I'm glad to see he's starting to say that the only real safe sex is no sex outside of marriage," Ryan said about Johnson. "But I have a problem with making a hero out of him because of AIDS."[50]

The idea that Nolan Ryan is a sex symbol, safe or otherwise, is not as outrageous a notion as some fans might think. In fact, in an unscientific poll conducted by the *Dallas Morning News* in 1991, fans in Texas rated Nolan Ryan the second sexiest man in all of sports, behind tennis idol Andre Agassi. "So smitten are you with Ryan," wrote sportswriter Barry Horn, "that you had the balding 44-year-old father of a college pitcher tied for second as the sexiest male athlete." (Ryan tied with quarterbacks Troy Aikman and Joe Montana.)[51]

Ryan himself has recognized that people see him as a sex symbol. "Because I stay in shape and have done some Wrangler Jeans ads," he said in *Miracle Man*, "some people call me a sex symbol for my age group. I don't view myself that way." And Ryan added that his status as sex symbol "bugs Ruth, and I suppose it would bother any wife to think her husband is being looked at by other women as some sort of object."[52]

No doubt it would bug both Ruth and Nolan to know that some men look at him "as some sort of object" too.[53]

Advertisers have capitalized on Ryan's image of safe sexuality. Some print and television advertisements, including those for Advil, Duracell batteries, Southwest Airlines, Starter apparel, and Whataburger, are relatively asexual, simply showing Ryan in his baseball uniform and referring to his status as athlete and major league pitcher. Other advertisements project an image-oriented appeal. For example, Ryan wore a business suit in his BizMart print advertisements, and he wore a tuxedo in the Bic television advertisements that aired on the three major networks during the fall of 1990. He also is seen in a tuxedo on the cover of *Miracle Man*. Still other ads are more sexual in their appeal. In the Wrangler Jeans print ad, he wears tight-fitting jeans, a cowboy shirt, a cowboy hat, and cowboy boots. Most striking, a print advertisement displayed in several issues of *Sports Illustrated, Esquire,* and other magazines in the early 1990s presented a close-up of Ryan's face and pitching hand, but the top of his balding head was cut out of the picture, and his face and hands were moistened so that they glistened in the sepia tones used to color the image. Although these and other images are not overtly sexual, they do reveal that advertisers have exploited (and manipulated) Ryan's physical appearance to sell their products.

Perhaps the most intriguing use of sexual imagery can be found in a poster titled "Texas Ranger" distributed by Nike. The poster shows Ryan standing in the middle of a dirt street on a Western set, a saddled horse is behind him on his right, and a wooden derrick stands to his left, near a sign that reads, "Pride, Texas." Ryan is dressed in a white Ranger baseball uniform, and he stands on a pitching "rubber." However, Ryan wears a long western overcoat over his uniform, and instead of a baseball cap, he sports a cowboy hat. Most impressively, Ryan wears a holster below his baseball uniform belt; but instead of holding guns, this holster holds baseballs, one on each side, though they are not quite symmetrically hung.

For those inclined to search for sexual symbolism—especially those influenced by Freudian analysis—Ryan's "Texas Ranger" poster is full of possibilities. One could interpret the long derrick at Ryan's left, placed next to the "Pride, Texas" sign, as a fairly obvious phallic symbol. Ryan's hat, a tall cowboy hat, could also be seen as a phallic symbol. Ryan's overcoat might symbolize a condom. And the not-quite-symmetrical baseballs in Ryan's holster could be symbolic of his testicles.[54] Conspicuously absent from the holster is a gun, another phallic symbol, or "penile extender," as Fiske called it.[55] But with a (base)ball on each side of his body and a rounded tip on the top of his head, the image is compelling, even to those skeptical of psychoanalytic theory: Ryan is the gun. Ryan is the phallus.

To say that Nolan Ryan is a male sex symbol is to say that he is a phallic symbol. And in his representation as a phallic symbol, Ryan stands very tall as he embodies traditional masculinity. "The promise of phallic power," argued Segal, "is precisely this guarantee of total inner coherence, of an unbroken and unbreakable, an unquestioned and unquestionable masculinity."[56] Ryan is the hard phallus, conditioned by years of rigorous exercise. Ryan is the true phallus, offered to only one woman, his beautiful and devoted wife. Ryan is the safe phallus, protected by an overcoat and performing on a pitching rubber. Perhaps most importantly, Ryan is the middle-aged phallus, still possessing the power to explode. As another Wrangler Jeans advertisement put it: "300 wins and he still hasn't lost the crease [or, by extension, the bulge] in his jeans." No wonder that on the day after Ryan threw his sixth no-hitter, at age forty-three, *USA Today* ran a front-page headline, "Great Day to Be 43," and celebrated the fact that "nearly 4 million 43-year-olds woke up feeling young."[57]

Nolan Ryan represents an attractive, white, middle-aged cowboy-banker-athlete with physical strength and rugged individualism who was raised by a middle-class family with working-class values in a small rural town, and who is a strong father and devoted husband. For white, middle-aged, middle-class, beer-drinking scribes interested in maintaining a traditional sense of masculinity, it doesn't get any better than this.

Taking the Gendering of Sports Seriously

The sports media reinforce a traditional sense of masculinity when they emphasize the power of the male athlete, the institution of familial patriarchy, the mythos of the frontiersman, and the symbolism of the phallus. When the media emphasize any one of these features, they reinforce a dimension of masculinity that has been adopted by most "mainstream" Americans. However, when they emphasize all of these features in combination, as they have done in coverage of Nolan Ryan, they reinforce the dominant gender ideology of American culture.

The importance of gender representations in the sports media should not be taken lightly. Feminist Lois Bryson argued that women who ignore sport do so at their own peril because "sport is a powerful institution through which male [dominance] is constructed and reconstructed and it is only through understanding and confronting these processes that we can hope to break this domination." In fact, she went so far as to say that "sport needs to be analyzed along with rape, pornography, and domestic violence as one of the means through which men monopolize physical force."[58] Thus, as Nolan Ryan's masculinity has been represented by the media, Ryan's image has come to symbolize not only athletic dominance over men, but also symbolic dominance over women. Not surprisingly then, the image of masculinity reinforced by coverage of Nolan Ryan challenges feminism. It seems safe to say that Nolan Ryan will never be asked to be a poster boy for the National Organization for Women.

The reinforcement of traditional masculinity through the sports media also has potential negative consequences for men. "In a world sadly consistent with the Hobbesian legacy," said two sociologists, "sports encourage men to forever compete with one another, never trusting and never feeling, and to regard women as frail underlings who are far removed from the panoply of patriarchical pugnacity and privilege."[59] This underscores the importance of examining how the mass media reinforce these and other values through their coverage of American sports figures like Nolan Ryan.

Conclusion: Nolan Ryan and American Values

Every major league baseball player means different things to different people. He is an athlete with unique abilities used strategically on the field by coaches and managers. He is a professional whose contracts are negotiated off the field by agents, franchise executives, and advertising representatives. He is a member of a high-profile entertainment industry whose game performances and career accomplishments are covered in detail by beat writers and broadcasters. He is a favorite player of an admiring group of fans who follow his career, collect his baseball cards, and select him in fantasy leagues. He is a neighbor, fishing buddy, or business partner for friends and acquaintances. He is a husband, father, son, and grandson to family members.

Although every player is an individual with special importance to those around him, a select group of players rise above the rest because of outstanding accomplishments, impressive careers, or unique personal attributes. Certainly, Nolan Ryan is such a player. With an on-the-field career that featured more than twenty-five major league seasons and fifty major league records and with an off-the-field life as a cowboy-banker-endorser, Nolan Ryan has special meaning in American culture.

As sportswriters and sportscasters covered Ryan's career, they also have presented certain images of American culture. Scholarly and popular writers alike have argued that sports reflect certain cultural values of American society. In this last chapter, I examine some broader sets of American values that have been reinforced in media coverage of Nolan Ryan.

Nolan Ryan and American Cultural Values

The American value system is complex and multidimensional. Sociologist Robin Williams has said that fifteen major value orientations have defined American culture in the last two hundred years: achievement, activity and work, efficiency, rationality, practicality, progress, material comfort, morality, equality, freedom, democracy, nationalism, individualism, humanitarianism, and group superiority. Similarly, psychologist Milton Rokeach has written that American society has been characterized by values such as ambition, honesty, courage, freedom, independence, accomplishment, salvation, and others.[1]

Given the complex and ever-changing nature of our society, it is not surprising that a variety of values, including some that seem to contradict each other, characterize American culture. At certain times, some values are stressed over others. During most wars, patriotic values, such as courage, cooperation, sacrifice, and nationalism, are emphasized by our leaders and our presses, while during times of economic boom, business values, such as achievement, work, materialism, and ambition, are emphasized. Virtually all of the time, some groups in society endorse one set of values while other groups endorse a competing set: consider, for example, the value differences expressed during Republican and Democratic conventions.

I conclude by examining some of the American values reinforced in media coverage of Nolan Ryan. Some of these values were suggested in preceding chapters as I discussed how the media have represented Ryan as hero, commodity, celebrity, and image of masculinity. Now I look at how, through Ryan, the media reinforced certain American values related to images of success and failure, work and play, youth and experience, teamwork and individualism, and tradition and change.

Success and Failure

"Nolan Ryan, a pitcher defined by great numbers, finally got the number that defines great pitchers."
                                                        —ASSOCIATED PRESS

The most dominant value reinforced in American sports is success. Sports sociologist Howard Nixon wrote that "sport seems to be an ideal vehicle for understanding the pursuit of the American Dream . . . because achievement and success are so openly and explicitly emphasized in sport."[2] Not surprisingly, most media coverage of sports defines success as winning. Baseball lore is filled with celebrated clichés about winning. George Steinbrenner said, "Winning is second only to breathing." Leo Durocher said, "Win any way you can as long as you can get away with it" and "Show me a good loser and I'll show you an idiot." Pete Rose said: "Creating success is tough. But keeping it is tougher. You have to keep producing, you can't ever stop. Not even to take a crap."[3]

In sports, as in business, success is measured statistically in bottom-line terms. "For Americans," observed Michael Novak, "nothing is real until it's counted."[4] The ultimate bottom line in baseball is found in the won-lost column of the sports pages. The rules of American baseball ensure that only one team can win each game, no matter how many innings it takes, (though ties are allowed and considered honorable in Japanese baseball), and every year, only one team can win each division, each pennant, and, ultimately, the World Series. Virtually every aspect of player and team performance is quantified by sabermetricians, but it is the won-lost record of the team that counts the most.

Critics argue convincingly that this preoccupation with (and quantification of) winning and losing constitutes a narrow definition of success and failure. Popular writer James Michener, for example, argued that success occurs even in losing "when the individual assesses the capacities allocated to him by his genetic inheritance and determines to use them to the best of his ability." In fact, shortly before Vince Lombardi died, he had misgivings about his infamous statement, "Winning isn't everything, it's the only thing," according to Michener. "He told Jerry Izenberg, 'I wish to hell I'd never said the damn thing. I meant the effort. . . . I meant having a goal. . . . I sure as hell didn't mean for people to crush human values and morality.'"[5]

Nevertheless, the importance of winning is reinforced by the sports media daily, even though the best teams in baseball lose at least one-third of their games in the regular season. And year after year, the sports media ultimately evaluate teams like the Seattle Mariners and Texas Rangers, which have never won a division title, and the Chicago Cubs and Cleveland Indians, which have developed bona fide traditions of losing, as failures, even though they may have displayed improvement on the field, development of young players, or stability in the front office.

Success and failure, then, are inevitable results in sports and inevitable themes in media coverage of sports. Both themes have featured prominently in coverage of Nolan Ryan.

Throughout Ryan's career, sportswriters have evaluated his success and failure as a major league pitcher. Because he was a pitcher, his individual won-lost record often was used to assess his success as a baseball player. As noted in the introduction to this book, Ryan's won-lost record hovered just above .500 for most of his career, and some sportswriters cited this won-lost record to conclude that Ryan was not a successful pitcher. Other sportswriters defended Ryan, pointing out that he played much of his career for weak franchises with terrible team won-lost records, and that Ryan gave these teams more wins than they could have enjoyed without him.

Over his career media gave mixed reports of Ryan's reaction to the criticism that he was little more than a .500 pitcher. When he signed as a million-dollar free agent with Houston, Mike Littwin of the *Los Angeles Times* quoted Ryan as saying that he was not bothered by his critics. "Maybe I've lost too many games to be considered a great pitcher," he said in an article. "But it's always bothered other people more than it's bothered me." Ryan also said that "I've always had critics," but "they don't bother me anymore."[6] A few years later, in 1983, Henry Hecht of the *New York Post* confirmed Ryan's reported indifference to the criticism. "I'm to the point where I don't really care what people's criticisms of me are," Ryan said, "whether they think I'm a good pitcher or not."[7]

Before the 1992 season, however, Frank Luksa of the *Dallas Morning News* wrote that Ryan was bitter about the criticism of his career record. "Ryan has heard the rap," Luksa said. "The subject bring him nearer to boil than any. His Texas twang takes a bite and snaps as he confronts the issue." The reporter then quoted Ryan's explanation: "Lots of it comes from people who don't like you. They stir you up to get a reaction. Or they're young people who don't know any better. A lot of it is sheer ignorance."[8]

Virtually all of Ryan's critics admitted, finally, that he was a genuinely successful pitcher after he won his 300th game, becoming only the twentieth pitcher in history to do so. Sportswriters unanimously acclaimed this milestone accomplishment and agreed that it represented a form of success that would ensure Ryan a spot in the Hall of Fame. In fact, Ryan's defenders used the milestone to criticize his former critics; as one put it, "No. 300 cuts their vocal chords."[9]

Clearly, the sports media reinforced the value of success and the importance of winning in covering Ryan's career. In a limited sense, the emphasis on winning reflects the fact that, in our capitalist society, business performance is judged ultimately by a measurable bottom line. And it reminds us that the American dream can be achieved only by "putting up the numbers."

Unfortunately, the sports media tend to overemphasize winning as the primary—and at times only—definition of success. This overemphasis is far too limited for a sports world that restricts winning to few teams and for a society that needs people who do not win to do the best job they can. Sadly, if workers are defined as truly successful only when they achieve incredible goals, as Ryan did when he won his 300th game, then people "are cast into ceaseless work and action to prove their worth," as critic John Fiske observed, and success "becomes almost a definition of the superhuman, so that it becomes that which can never [or at best rarely] be achieved."[10] If we really believe that Nolan Ryan was successful only because he won his 300th game, then the vast majority of ballplayers and at least 99 percent of the rest of us are destined to live our lives as "failures."

Work and Play

*"Ryan puts in three hours of preparation for every one hour the
other Texas pitchers spend. 'That's the price you pay to be Nolan
Ryan,' [Tom House, his former pitching coach] said."*

—Los Angeles Times

Another paradoxical set of values reinforced by the sports
media is that of work and play. Sportswriters often remind readers that
professional sport is hard work. "Athletes often are well aware that what
they do is not play," wrote William Sadler. "Their practice sessions are
workouts; and to win the game they have to work harder."[11]

Critics have argued that professional sport has become a form of in-
dustrialized and highly mechanized labor. Jean-Marie Brohm wrote that
"sport is basically a mechanization of the body, treated as an automaton,
governed by the principle of maximizing output." Brohm went on to suggest that sport "requires the Taylorization of the body," referring to Frederick Taylor's principles of "scientific management," which put a premium
on maximum productivity achieved through efficient work methods and
structures.[12]

Yet sport also reflects the value of play and the so-called Leisure Ethic.
After all, sport has its roots in games that are played and watched for
fun and enjoyment. "Sports are played and watched," wrote psychiatrist
Arnold Beisser, "for pleasure, for the joy of exuberant movement of the
body, for diversion from the tedium of life, and for the display before
others."[13] Sportswriters who write about the enjoyment that athletes or
fans experience from the game and from the camaraderie with their teammates or other fans reinforce this value of play.

For the most part, sportswriters have focused on Nolan Ryan's hard
work in sports, epitomized by their attention to his "almost perfect"
mechanics and "legendary" workouts. "Through studious devotion to
mechanics," said one conditioning expert in *Newsweek*, "Ryan has gotten maximum efficiency from his physical output." As described in
Chapter 3, Ryan's dedication to his workouts has been presented in similarly mechanistic terms. "He is as punctual as he is hardworking," said
sportswriter David Casstevens. "On days he pitches he arrives at the
park three hours early, like clockwork. . . . 'The routine,' he said, 'never
varies.'"[14]

In one surprising report, Tom House, Ryan's pitching coach for the
Rangers until 1993, was mildly critical of Ryan's machine-like obsession
with his workouts, suggesting that Ryan may have been working too hard
for his own good. "I'm convinced Nolan has been overtraining all his life,"
he said. "Nolan believes so strongly in the hard work ethic that the idea

of active rest is foreign to him. The hard work is important. It's the key, but you have to give your body time to regroup."[15]

Unfortunately, in dwelling on Ryan's work, sportswriters de-emphasized the playful aspects of Ryan's career. A few token stories about Ryan enjoying himself were presented: while with the Angels, Ryan gave a fan named Frank a chance to hit against him before a game. As an Astro, Ryan mimicked the growl of Cincinnati Reds' pitcher Brad "The Animal" Lesley after striking out one of his teammates. But stories of playful moments in Ryan's career were few and far between.

Some sportswriters suggested that Ryan was too committed to the work of pitching to enjoy the game of baseball. When teammates celebrated his strikeout records and no-hitters in the clubhouse after the game with beer and champagne, reporters noted that Ryan was riding a stationary bike, not deviating from "the routine." Frank Luksa quoted Ryan as saying he does not even enjoy looking back on his memorable strikeout records and no-hit games: "'Pitching to me is a high-intensity exercise and commitment,' he said. 'I have to get to such a level of intensity and aggressiveness that I don't look back on games as the greatest thing in my life. . . . I'm too intense to enjoy them.'"[16]

By overemphasizing his work and underemphasizing his play, the sports media represented Ryan as a superhuman machine who only works, not as a normal human being who occasionally plays. "Ryan operates beyond the reach of physical laws," exaggerated one writer.[17] The media unwittingly revealed Ryan to be the perfect illustration of the "Taylorization" of the body critiqued by Brohm.

A print advertisement for Duracell batteries offered the most vivid mechanistic image: Ryan is shown in his uniform, grimacing as he delivers a pitch; the caption reads, "He runs like he's on Duracell." But as we see him grimace in an effort to keep the Ryan machine running, we know that his batteries cannot last forever and that when they finally run out, they cannot be replaced. When they finally do run out, will Nolan Ryan be able to look back and enjoy his career?

Youth and Experience

"The man has a forty-one-year-old arm that's livelier than any rookie's. No theory accounts for it, or even predicts its eventual end."
—GENTLEMEN'S QUARTERLY

Both the value of youth and that of experience are reinforced by members of the sports media. Reporters and broadcasters admire the young ballplayer, especially the rookie, because he is said to exhibit strength, speed, agility, and other valued physical qualities, as well as desire, eagerness, enjoyment, and other valued psychological qualities. But they also tell us that the rookie is raw, impatient, and undeveloped because he lacks experience. On the other hand, older players are supposed to be seasoned leaders who exhibit wisdom, patience, maturity, and even guile to help the club win games. However, the veteran's physical skills are said to have deteriorated and, in some cases, he is described as "burned out." Members of the sports media agree that, given their complementary nature, both youth and experience are needed for a successful season.

Although sportswriters agree that both are essential to team success, the value of youth has dominated American culture, especially in the mass media. "The dominant icon of consumer culture," wrote critic John Hargreaves, "is the youthful, sexually attractive, healthy, physically fit person." He concluded that "the cultural imperative to all" of us, regardless of age or gender, is to "look, act, and feel as if we are" young. Most of our entertainment programs, commercials, and even newscasts are filled with young adults who have attractive faces, shapely bodies, and, of course, good hair. And it is easy to predict that readers of *Sports Illustrated* will never find an elderly or endomorphic model in their annual swimsuit edition. As Hargreaves concluded, "To be sportive is almost by definition to be desirable, fit, young, and healthy."[18]

Members of the media have emphasized youth and experience in different ways as they covered Ryan's career. For the most part, they have endorsed the value of youth by focusing on Ryan's unique ability as a power pitcher to throw the ball hard as a raw rookie and then as a middle-aged "miracle man." Even though Ryan credited the development of a slower change-up as crucial to his continued success, the media remained fixated on his youthful ability to "throw heat" in the mid-90 MPH range after all those years.

Sportswriters also have emphasized the value of experience as they presented Ryan as a veteran who played with teammates and for managers who were much younger than he was. When nineteen-year-old catcher Ivan Rodriguez caught the forty-four-year-old Ryan in a near no-hitter against the Angels, the Associated Press story began with the lead: "Texas catcher Ivan Rodriguez was learning to walk when Nolan Ryan threw his first no-hitter." Frank Luksa joked that "Ryan can never seem to pitch for someone his age," commenting on the hiring of Ranger manager Kevin Kennedy, who, like his predecessor, Bobby Valentine, is younger than Ryan. And the same writer joked about Ryan's point of view in another story: "The Rangers' locker room must appear like a kindergarten to Ryan. All that is missing are swing sets and monkey bars. Or a sand box."[19]

Sportswriter Phil Rogers, on the other hand, described the benefit of Ryan's many years in the majors: "Experience has allowed Ryan a rare perspective. He understands what forces he can control and what he cannot control, and satisfies himself to keep his team in a game he is pitching, regardless of the outcome."[20]

In the final analysis, I believe that the sports media have overemphasized the value of youth through Nolan Ryan. Sportswriters suggested that Ryan somehow was defeating the aging process with his ability to "throw heat" into his thirties and forties, calling him "the ageless wonder" and "miracle man." One headline said simply that his "flame burns eternal." This surprising claim was quoted in another story: "'I was watching him (on television) and he hasn't even aged,' said Joe Saladino, . . . a longtime friend of Ryan's. 'He looks the same as he did when he was 18.'" No surprise, then, that Arlington Stadium loudspeakers often played Rod Stewart's song "Forever Young" when Ryan took to the mound.[21]

These and other symbolic expressions of Ryan's "eternal youth" make me wonder if Ryan, as baseball's Dorian Gray, kept a Nike poster of himself in the storm cellar of his ranch, letting it age for him. Commenting on Ryan's ability to throw the ball hard, as well as his average won-lost record, one reporter joked that "Ryan, in exchange for the gift of speed, conceded the Devil not his soul but the ability to win baseball games."[22]

These and other images of Ryan's agelessness made for clever headlines and feature stories, but these stories also reinforced some negative lessons about the importance of youth in society. His wholesome way of life was usually described not as a way of keeping healthy but rather a way of keeping young. Ryan's workouts were described by some as obsessions motivated by a desire to defeat time. "The ticking clock of Father Time," wrote one reporter, "has turned Ryan's workouts into obsessions." Another feature indicated that Ryan's workouts were driven by the decision that Ryan made "as a young man, that he never wanted to look paunchy, be out of shape or lose his athletic abilities by his early 30s."[23] It is not surprising, then, that advertising consultants for Wrangler placed Ryan on the mound in a pair of tight-fitting jeans for their print advertisements. As one reporter aptly summarized Ryan's importance in American culture, he is "one of the most celebrated athletes of our time and an icon to a public preoccupied with retaining its youth."[24]

Time magazine insisted that Ryan's "eternal youth" was inspiring for those in their middle and advanced ages. "Nolan Ryan's never ending glory is inspiration for the geezers," the featured concluded. "What man in his 40s would not like to look in the mirror and find Nolan Ryan?"[25] However, in presenting Ryan as a superman obsessed enough to maintain the power and strength of his youth through machine-like dedication to his workouts, the media have given us a role model for inspiration, but certainly not for emulation. After all, only one man can look in the mirror and see Nolan Ryan. And if others who played with Ryan could not maintain their power and strength with age, how can we have even the slightest chance of doing so?

I wonder, with some apprehension, how the media will portray Nolan Ryan ten and twenty years from now when his batteries have run out and when he will not quite fit into a cape and tight jeans. When he can no longer throw heat, not even in an old-timers' game, what kind of "inspiration for geezers" will he be presented as in the media?

Teamwork and Individualism

"Ryan projects an image of rugged individualism, but admits to taking more comfort in being part of a team."
                                    —DALLAS TIMES HERALD

Teamwork and individualism constitute another pair of American values that receive attention in the sports media. Teamwork is described as a commitment to the ideal that the good of the team is more important than the good of any individual player. As one observer put it, "Loyalty, unity, affiliation, and the ability to place the good of the group above one's own interests are basic constituents of the sports world's ethic."[26]

Yet individualism is also valued in American sports, especially in baseball. "A characteristic that distinguishes baseball from its major competitors is that it is more individualistic," wrote Leon Warshay. "Despite the fact that teamwork is required, in most game conditions there is still a premium on individual skill and identity." Michael Novak concurred that "In baseball . . . [t]he fundamental unit is the individual," and he concluded that "the most highly developed state of the individual is to be a good 'team player,' to encourage and assist his fellows" and "to 'hold up his end,' 'not let them down.'"[27]

Media coverage of Nolan Ryan reinforced the values of both teamwork and individualism. Reporters often described Ryan as a team player. On the field, Ryan was shown as committed to helping his team win. "I think my job is to give my team a chance to win the ballgame when I pitch," he said before his first season with the Rangers. "If I do that, I am happy, regardless whether I get the win or somebody else gets the win."[28] In the same article, Ryan was openly critical of players lacking a team attitude: "I think you see less of that [team] attitude today in baseball than you ever have. . . . Players know their earning power is tied to statistics. I don't look at it that way."

A few years later, as Ryan remained winless two months into the 1992 season, having several leads blown by the Ranger bullpen, he repeated the same message to Randy Galloway: "'Frustration for me comes only if we lose the game,' said Ryan. 'Anytime a pitcher puts that personal 'W' ahead of the final score, then he's got a problem. . . . As long as I can give us a chance to win, that's the ultimate achievement.'"[29]

Ryan also was portrayed as an unofficial team leader in the clubhouse, even though he was never the official team captain. *Sports Illustrated* described him as the "ideal complement to the Rangers' young starters . . . who can learn from him." However, Gerry Fraley suggested that Ryan was a "naturally reserved" leader who "does not seek out teammates and tell them what to do. If they want help, they must observe."[30]

Members of the media have also emphasized Ryan's individualism. Clearly, they celebrated his individual accomplishments and personality by presenting him as an American hero. They also celebrated his individual earning power as an on-the-field commodity and as an off-the-field celebrity-endorser who deserved every penny he received. But reporters also presented a different sense of Ryan's individualism when they revealed that he received special treatment from the franchises for which he played. "Some of the Angel teammates aren't happy with the Angels' special considerations for Ryan," revealed Dick Miller in *The Sporting News*. "'They treat him differently than the rest of us,' said one player who asked that his name not be used." Years later, Ruben Sierra of the Rangers made a similar complaint when he said, "I'm a great player too. But everything's 'Nolan, Nolan' around here."[31]

Ryan admitted in *Miracle Man* that he enjoyed the special treatment he received from the Rangers: "I was surprised as anybody with my popularity and the attention I received, but the Rangers were the first organization to put me out front and promote me like that. . . . I somehow became more of a phenomenon in Arlington than I had been in Houston, because the Astro organization never would have pushed me or appreciated me the way the Rangers have."[32]

In sum, sportswriters have emphasized both teamwork and individualism in their coverage of Ryan, and in so doing, they have revealed some of the natural tensions between these two American values. Through Ryan, the media strongly challenged the individualism of selfish teammates who seek personal goals on the field in order to increase their own salaries. Through the few players bold enough to criticize Ryan, the media mildly challenged the self-interested franchises that give special treatment to individual players in order to increase attendance and also to athletes who would expect such special treatment. But because they presented Ryan as a team-oriented hero, it is clear that sportswriters were willing to endorse Ryan's special treatment. However, the media reaffirmed the fact that you have to be a player of Ryan's caliber to deserve special treatment.

Tradition and Change

"[Ryan] is an old-fashioned country ballplayer, a millionaire more comfortable in pickup trucks than limos."
                                                                —NEWSWEEK

A final pair of American values that find reaffirmation in sports and the media are tradition and change. Romantics who write about the national pastime, epitomized by the late Renaissance scholar and baseball commissioner A. Bartlett Giamatti, tell us that baseball tradition teaches us history lessons about the simple rural values of nation's past. Some celebrate the pastoral qualities of baseball, as George Grella did when he wrote that it reminds "us of our agricultural heritage, of the homely handicrafts of the past, when the land was the entire source for all the needed implements of the game."[33] Others have glorified the timelessness of the game, as Roger Angell did when he wrote: "Within the ballpark, time moves differently, marked by no clock except the events of the game. This is the unique unchangeable feature of baseball, and it perhaps ex- plains why this sport, for all the enormous changes it has undergone in the past decade or two, remains somehow rustic, unviolent, and introspec- tive."[34] And others have reminisced about the "golden age" of sports when there were genuine heroes like Lou Gehrig and Joe DiMaggio.

On the other hand, it is obvious that professional sports have changed dramatically and that they reflect changes in the values of American so- ciety. Many critics charge that the changes made in baseball reflect the abandoning of important social values of the past. "Modern baseball play- ers have changed," said Ralph Andreano over twenty years ago. Even though players in the past also liked to make money, Andreano argued, "ballplayers of an early era were more interested in the 'game' and not in the money."[35] The same can be said about some members of the sports media who seem to pay as much attention to the salaries of the players as to the game.

Of course, not all the changes in baseball have corrupted the values of the game. Some believe that although players' salaries have risen too much, the rise of free agency liberated players from what essentially had been a slave labor system. New technologies and training methods also have produced players who are stronger and more conditioned and who enjoy longer careers. And despite the alleged evils of television, that me- dium has brought the game of baseball to an audience of millions.

Media coverage of Nolan Ryan's career emphasized both tradition and change. Most memorable was the celebration of Ryan as a "hero of old" who represented the traditional values of the rural town of Alvin, Texas, where he was raised and still lives. Pete Axthelm wrote in *Newsweek* in 1985 that "Ryan has always brought to mind words like throwback and nature, writers like Grantland Rice and Ring Lardner." Another reporter wrote that "the values and mores inherent in a small town define Ryan, and in that regard, Alvin and Ryan are a perfect match."[36]

As I described in Chapter 3, the media have presented Ryan as repre- senting such timeless rural values as hard work, loyalty, humility, whole- someness, and commitment to family. As I suggested in Chapter 5, though, the media also have presented Ryan as representing an outdated sense of patriarchy as the lone breadwinner and protecting husband. The media presented these traditional values of Ryan's rural background as so important that he was quoted as saying that "living in Alvin, I think . . . probably prolonged my career."[37] But the media also have portrayed Ryan as a progressive player, willing to change. Ryan was one of the first pitchers to use weight training, which probably prolonged his career more than living in rural Texas did. Ryan used and endorsed many of Ranger coach Tom House's nontraditional training exercises, such as "underloading" (pitching with a lighter baseball to develop faster arm speed) and throwing footballs (because only with the proper delivery can one throw a spiral pass).

Ryan has been depicted as a ballplayer who represented modern-day values off the field as well, with his numerous commercial endorsements and book contracts. As discussed in Chapter 4, Ryan changed his own set of values regarding commercial endorsements. When he was an Angel, he accepted few endorsement opportunities because he wanted to "spend more time with [his] family," but when he was a Ranger, he accepted many endorsement opportunities because he wanted to "do more things for [his] family." Somewhat ironically, the media reported that Ryan has been such an attractive commercial spokesman because of the traditional values he has been said to represent.

Members of the media have endorsed the values of tradition and change in their coverage of Ryan. In representing Ryan as the rural cowboy with a commitment to traditional values, the media convincingly portrayed him as a genuine hero of a past era. But in presenting Ryan as the commercial endorser with a vested interest in cashing in on his fame, they revealed that he ultimately is a celebrity who reflects the capitalistic values of contemporary consumer culture. As Richard Gaughran, a scholar of baseball literature, put it, "Pastoral values can be realized only in the imagination, never for very long in the real world."[38]

As members of the sports media cover various teams and players over the years, they invariably invoke a wide variety of cultural values, emphasizing some and de-emphasizing others. In covering Nolan Ryan's lengthy career, reporters and broadcasters emphasized aspects of at least five sets of American values: success and failure, work and play, youth and experience, teamwork and individualism, and tradition and change. Undoubtedly, they reinforced aspects of additional value sets as well, including reason and emotion, logic and luck, mechanism and humanism, conformity and deviance, spirituality and secularism, and others. After all, baseball and its media coverage have many cultural meanings, as many as can be imagined by "the green fields of the mind."[39] Our challenge as baseball fans is to reflect on these and other aspects of American culture that are being reinforced in our sports pages and on our sports newscasts as we check for scores and stats. In so doing, we can become more enlightened students of the game and of our society.

Appendix

NOLAN RYAN PRESS CONFERENCE

AUGUST 22, 1989, 10:25 P.M.
ARLINGTON STADIUM

RYAN: I really don't have a statement, and I guess what we'll do is open it to questions. Maybe I can answer a few of them before we start. I'm relieved that it's over with. I'm disappointed that we didn't win tonight. I think that the game tonight was probably a reflection of why Oakland has been where they are all year. They have good pitching, and they're a good ballclub. So, hopefully, tomorrow, we'll come out and get headed in the right direction because as I said earlier, I feel like this is a big week for us. It was a big day for me. I'm relieved it's over with. I hope that the event wasn't a distraction to my teammates tonight because I know that it's hard not to let something like that affect you. I know that the first few innings, I felt the effects of it. I think I was overthrowing, and I didn't get into the groove that I did later in the game until about the third or fourth inning. I settled down and started throwing the ball a little better.

Q1: Before you go out to the mound after twenty-two years, do you still get butterflies at a moment like this?

RYAN: I was very nervous today. In fact, coming down the interstate, I drove right by the ballpark, to show you where my mind was. I had to turn around and come back. Yeah, I get nervous. I had to laugh at the All-Star game when I warmed up to come in to relieve behind Dave Stewart and I sat down to wait for the inning to get over and come in. And Greg Swindel and some of the young pitchers were sitting there, and they all turned around and looked at me and said, "Are you nervous?" I said, "Yeah, I'm not going to lie to you. I am nervous." I think that's the competitiveness in people that if they didn't get nervous and get up for what they're were doing, they wouldn't be so good.

Q2: Can you put this into perspective how it relates to your career. It's a great personal achievement, but . . . (pause)

RYAN: Well, (smiling) you know, I don't know. I'm disappointed that we lost. I saw Steve Carlton strike out nineteen and get beat 2-1 that one time against the Mets when Ron Swoboda hit the home run. You're excited about what you've accomplished, but in the end you're a little bit disappointed that it didn't end on a more positive note. That's the way I feel about it.

Q3: You came pretty close in the fourth inning to getting the record. Did you get kind of frustrated?

RYAN: No, I wasn't frustrated at all. I think that when I got two strikes on those guys, their approach to hitting me was a little different. I think they were going to make sure they put the bat on the ball. I think if you look at the balls that they hit, you know, they pretty much hit the ball where it was thrown. They were ground balls, whatever. I heard that before the game those guys had a pool about who it was gonna be, and I'm sure none of them wanted to be number 5,000. I'm sure Rickie didn't. In that situation, I got 3-2 on him and made a good pitch, and he was swinging the bat.

Q4: Would you say that this game was kind of a microcosm of your career?

RYAN: Well, I don't know. I hadn't thought about it. You know, it's disappointing when we lose.

Q5: When you were about to surpass Walter Johnson's record, you said you'd been a power pitcher all your life and you were going to stick to that. Have you ever changed your mind about that?

RYAN: No. You know, I've been fortunate to be able to maintain my stuff and be a power pitcher. I'm glad tonight that 5,000 came on a fastball. You know, at my age, if I lose my velocity, then I'm out of the game. I go year by year anyway. I'm not going to develop some new pitch that all of a sudden will keep me around for an extended period of time. I've benefitted over the last four or five years with the fact that my change-up is getting better. It makes me that much more of an effective pitcher. I established my curveball early tonight, then went to the change-up around the fourth inning and then threw a few curveballs. That makes me more effective with three pitches versus two. If I'm not getting one over, then I don't become a one-pitch pitcher.

Q6: Nolan, are you happy you got 5,000 with a fastball?

RYAN: Yeah, you know, if somebody had asked before the game, "What pitch would you like to have it on?" I'd like to have it on a fastball because that is my bread and butter pitch, and that's what got me to the big leagues, and that's what has made my other pitches effective. You work off your fastball.

Q7: When you look back on all your strikeouts, where will this one be?

RYAN: Well, of all the strikeouts—the Johnson record, the 4,000—this is the most meaningful, I think, because I did it later. To be honest with you, as a professional athlete—the response of the crowd tonight, the way the fans have treated me here—you know, I've been real fortunate. This year, twice, that's happened to me: going back to Anaheim, the night that I pitched against the Angels out there, and then tonight. As a professional athlete, that's a real special feeling because you strive to win and you strive to be the best you can and when your local fans come out and are appreciative of your efforts, then that's real rewarding.

Q8: Nolan, everybody is talking about your arm and how great your arm is, but no one I've asked knows how long it is. Do you know how long it is?

RYAN: Well, I wear a 34, 35 inch sleeve. When I get fitted for a suit (some laughs), they end up tailoring my right sleeve about an inch longer than the other. And it's not because my arm is longer, it's because my shoulder—it's my posture from throwing all these years. I'm not real correct or erect.

Q9: Nolan, on a year-to-year basis, as you say you've taken it, do you surprise yourself each year you come out and you still have your great fastball.

RYAN: Well, I guess. I know when I was younger, you always went to spring training with the thought in the back of your mind, "Well, are you going to start losing something off your fastball?" I have lost something off my fastball, but my control has gotten better, and my other pitches have gotten better. I think I'm convinced now—and probably have felt this way for several years—that I'm not going to wake up one day and not be able to throw hard. I think there will be factors that come into play that will keep me from pitching and from being effective, say my legs or just a breakdown of my body or have an injury or something. But to just wake up one day and not be able to throw hard again? I don't think that'll happen. I think I anticipated possibly that happening as a younger player because you always heard these nightmares that happened to people. But I don't think that's the case.

Q10: Does that mean you're going for 6,000?

RYAN: (smiling) No. But I don't make any predictions. I never thought I'd be standing here today. At forty-two years old, 6,000 is not realistic. You know, as far as next year is concerned, I'll have to make a decision on that before too long and see if I'm going to come back.

Q11: Nolan, how important will that 300th victory be?

RYAN: Well, you know, I tell people numbers aren't important to me, and I don't get motivated by numbers. If I come back next year and I'm within a reasonable shot of 300 wins, that would become a goal of mine, just as 5,000 was this year. I felt like if I pitched enough innings this year, I might have a shot at 5,000. But coming over here to Arlington to a new circumstance, I didn't know how many innings I was going to pitch, I didn't know how the heat was going to affect me, I didn't know the changes in the league, and I would have to learn the new hitters. I really didn't know what to expect as far as my effectiveness in the league this year. And I had no way of gauging strikeouts. So, I felt like if I pitched enough innings that I might have a shot at it this year.

Q12: You had mentioned that you didn't want the game stopped after you'd reached 5,000, but it seems the fans sort of stopped the game for you. What were you thinking when you were walking back to the mound and you were hearing that tremendous ovation.

RYAN: (smiling softly) Well, that's a special feeling, and it's hard to describe. I was relieved it was over with. It was nice that my teammates came in and congratulated me. I think in a situation like that, probably nobody really knows how to act. So, my attitude is, "Hey, we got a game to try to win here. And let's go on with it."

Q13: Any special messages for your fans and friends back in Alvin?

RYAN: Well, a lot of them have come up, and I appreciate that and the interest. I got a lot of phone calls, and I have a lot of telegrams in my locker from people that didn't come. I appreciate their support. They've always been very supportive of me. They've made living there very enjoyable.

Q14: You also set another Ranger record tonight, surpassing Fergie Jenkins in strikeouts, and this all happened in the fifth inning. Would you like to embark on that a little bit.

RYAN: Now that you mention that, I'm aware of that, but I wasn't really aware of it at the time. You know, I guess it's nice the first year you're here to break some of the pitching records. Hopefully I can add to that before the year is out.

Q15: Nolan, do you think anybody will ever reach 5,000 again?

RYAN: Well, I feel like that's a possibility. I mean, if I can accomplish that, who's to say that there might be a young pitcher that's coming in now that may have the longevity and the type of stuff that it takes. But, you know, it takes a combination of maintaining your stuff for an extremely long period of time and then staying healthy and pitching a lot of innings. You have to pitch a lot of innings. So this record consists of really two aspects: maintaining your stuff and then also staying healthy and pitching for such a long period of time that you pile enough innings.

Q16: Nolan, you mentioned you were trying to stay focused on the game after you got 5,000. Do you think that's the message that Bobby was trying to send when he came out there and got thrown out?

RYAN: Well, I really don't know what led to that ejection. I know that Bobby was saying something to the umpire and the umpire turned around and responded, and then Bobby said something else and he threw him out. I don't know what it was because I had been down in the clubhouse. I go down to stretch between innings, and I was coming back when all that took place. So, I didn't even bother with it.

Q17: Nolan, having reached 5,000 strikeouts and with so many peaks in your career, do you have any other goals, personal or otherwise.

RYAN: Well, I don't set number goals. My goal here was to help this ball-club win a pennant, and that's still a goal of mine, and hopefully we can bounce back and get right back in this race and maybe achieve that.

Q18: If the Rangers don't make a miracle comeback this year, would that be enough of a reason to come back next year to have a chance to win one?

RYAN: Well, you know, the first thing that weighs on my mind in making a decision like that is our family. This is the first time we've been away from home for nine years. So, it's the first time these kids have had to deal with this situation. If they're comfortable with it and want to do it, and if I feel that I can come back and contribute next year and put that behind us, then certainly . . . I feel like the Ranger organization certainly has taken the right attitude about improving the ballclub. I think they realize that there are still areas that we can improve upon. If they have that same attitude they had before this year, then I think certainly we'll be in a position to be a contender next year, so that may be a factor.

Q19: Nolan, as much as we'd like to see you do this forever, we know better, and we talked about that earlier tonight. Frank Giles says you're not the coaching type. What do you see in your future after pitching?

RYAN: Well, I don't see myself staying in uniform on the major-league level. I see myself staying involved in baseball to some degree whether it be with youth or with minor league operations. I don't really know. You don't do something as long as I have and be so involved in it that you just walk away from it. Then again, I've never had a summer off so I don't know how I'm going to deal with that. There's going to have to be an adjustment with my life when I get out of the game. So, as far as me making any kind of predictions, I don't know how I'm going to handle that. I'm sure that the adjustment will be there.

Q20: Nolan, the first five strikeouts seemed to come pretty quickly but the last one—you had three full counts, a couple of foul balls, maybe a questionable call in there. Did you begin to wonder about that one?

RYAN: No, I think that, you know, at that point in time that early in the game, I'm not concerned about when it's going to come. If I'm throwing that way in the middle innings like that, I feel that I have a reasonable shot at it. I certainly didn't want it to come on a questionable call. And I think with two strikes some of the hitters' approach to hitting me changed. I think they just wanted to put the ball in play. You know, I've been in that position. I was in that position with Pete Rose on the National League hit record. If you can evade that situation, you certainly want to. There's not a professional athlete out there that wanted to go down as number 5,000. (Reporters laugh) I'm sure Rickie doesn't feel nearly as bad about it now as he probably thought he would if it were him prior to the game.

Q21: Have you spoken to Henderson?

RYAN: I saw him over in the dugout just for a second. He was getting ready to go on HSE. (Reporters laugh.) He didn't seem to be bitter about it.

Q22: What did you tell him?

RYAN: (smiling) I told him, I says, "Rickie, somebody had to be 5,000. Sorry it was you. But that's the way it works out." (Reporters laugh.) There isn't a whole lot you can say. I appreciate it, I guess.

Q23: Nolan, we've heard a lot about the several players that you've struck out consistently or the most. Who's the hardest player over your career?

RYAN: I get that question a lot and there's really not one person I can say because of the length of time that we're talking about. I can remember in certain years that certain guys gave me trouble. I think overall I hated to see Pete Rose come to the plate with a guy in scoring position or a guy on third with less than two outs, because he was such a competitor, and he would foul off pitches that he couldn't hit, and he'd make you work so hard. You just never knew about Pete. But I faced Pete for an extended period of time because of the longevity in his career. But it varies. I remember one year that at the end of a season with the Angels that somebody asked, "Who did you strike out the most?" I said, "Well, I don't know really who it was, but it seemed to me that I struck Sal Bando out a lot," which I did that year. And I'll be darned, next year, it seemed like I couldn't get him out. So, I don't make statements like that any more. (Reporters laugh.)

Q24: Where do you see your place in baseball history?

RYAN: I don't know. You know, I don't think about those things. My attitude is, I just concern myself with what's going on in getting ready for my next start. In the morning, I'll get up and be back over here in the weight room getting ready for the Angels on Sunday. And this will be behind me. I'm sure someday, when it's all said and done, that I'll reflect back on it.

Q25: Nolan, have you ever been to the Hall of Fame?

RYAN: Yeah, I went with the Astros when we played Boston in the Hall of Fame game. And I know as players, we saw one of our off days was scheduled for that, and we weren't too enthused about it. But after I went up there, I was really thankful that I got that opportunity because it was very pleasant and I really enjoyed it. I don't know anybody that plays the game that wouldn't enjoy going up there and being involved in the festivities.

Q26: How are you going to feel about being elected in?

RYAN: Well, if I get elected to it or voted in it will be, if not the highlight, then, one of the highlights of my career. I think it's probably like what I call the honor that the fans gave me tonight. It will be that type of feeling.

Q27: (inaudible)

RYAN: No, it didn't really matter to me. I'm glad it worked out like it did. I'm disappointed we didn't win.

Ryan pauses, then says, "All right, well, thank you." Reporters applaud as Ryan leaves the press conference.

Notes

Introduction

1. Seymour Siwoff, Steve Hirdt, Tom Hirdt, and Peter Hirdt, *The 1991 Elias Baseball Analyst*, pp. 52–53.

2. Bill James, *The Bill James Historical Baseball Abstract*, p. 420.

3. Craig R. Wright and Tom House, *The Diamond Appraised*, p. 192.

4. Bill James, *The Baseball Book of 1992*, p. 29.

5. David Quentin Voigt, *American through Baseball*, p. 188; Steven A. Riess, *Touching Base: Professional Baseball and American Culture in the Progressive Era*, p. 5.

6. Susan Tyler Eastman and Timothy P. Meyer, "Sports Programming: Scheduling, Costs, and Competition," in *Media, Sports, and Society*, ed. Lawrence A. Wenner, pp. 97–119; David A. Klatell and Norman Marcus, *Sports for Sale: Television, Money and the Fans*, p. 26. For other discussions of the sports media industry, see Paul D. Staudohar and James A. Mangan, eds., *The Business of Professional Sports*, and James Edward Miller, *The Baseball Business: Pursuing Pennants and Profits in Baltimore*.

7. Allen Guttmann, *Sports Spectators*, p. 141. Also see Benjamin G. Rader, *In Its Own Image: How Television Has Transformed Sports*, pp. 138–55.

8. William O. Johnson, *Super Spectators and the Electric Lilliputians*, p. 103.

9. Rick Telander, "The Written Word: Player-Press Relationships in American Sports," *Sociology of Sport Journal* 1 (1984): 5–6.

10. Ibid., p. 5.

11. Richard Lipsky, *Sportsworld: An American Dreamland*, p. 351; Harry Edwards, *The Sociology of Sport*, p. 90. See also Howard L. Nixon, *Sport and the American Dream*.

12. Both quotes are from Michael S. Kimmel, "Baseball and the Reconstitution of American Masculinity," in *Cooperstown Symposium on Baseball and the American Culture, 1989*, ed. Alvin L. Hall, p. 288.

13. The Roosevelt quote is from Kimmel, ibid., p. 288; the Herbert Hoover quote is from Michael Novak, *The Joy of Sports*, p. 1.

14. Quoted in Novak, *Joy of Sports*, p. 1.

15. John Hargreaves, "Sport and Hegemony: Some Theoretical Problems," in *Sport, Culture, and the Modern State*, ed. Hart Cantelon and Richard Gruneau, p. 128.

Chapter 1

1. I describe Ryan's media coverage in four phases that correspond to the periods of time he spent with each of his teams: the New York Mets (1966–71), the California Angels (1972–79), the Houston Astros (1980–88), and the Texas Rangers (1989–93). This review is based on an examination of more than five hundred articles from popular print media, including newspapers (e.g., the *New York Times*, *Los Angeles Times*, *Dallas Morning News*, and *Houston Post*) and magazines (general ones such as *Life*, *Time*, *Newsweek*, and *Saturday Evening Post* and sports-oriented ones such as *Sport*, *Sports Illustrated*, and *The Sporting News*). The dates of these print materials span the period from 1965, the year before Ryan made his major league debut with the Mets, through 1993, the year Ryan completed his record twenty-seventh season of major league baseball at the age of forty-six.

2. Leonard Koppett, "Ryan, McGraw Are Losers in 9-2 and 6-5 Decisions," *New York Times*, Sept. 19, 1966.

3. Jack Lang, "Ryan Whiff Saga a Myth," *The Sporting News*, July 1, 1967, p. 16; Leonard Koppett, "Atlanta Routs Ribant in Taking Third Straight, 8-3," *New York Times*, Sept. 12, 1966.

4. "Brine for Nolan Ryan," *Life*, May 31, 1968, p. 78.

5. "These Are the Mets, Champions All," *New York Times*, Oct. 17, 1969; Murray Chass, "Pepitone Clouts Four-Run Homer," *New York Times*, June 11, 1970.

6. Ross Newhan, "Nolan Ryan: Four Years Is Too Long to Be a 'Prospect,'" *Los Angeles Times*, Feb. 28, 1972.

7. John Strege, "Heat and Humility," *Orange County Register*, June 16, 1992.

8. Joseph Durso, "Mets Down Cubs, 4-0, as Ryan Hurls 3 Hitter and Fans 13," *New York Times*, Aug. 5, 1970.

9. Jack Lang, "Ryan—Trade Him or Wait?" *Star Ledger*, Mar. 19, 1971.

10. Al Harvin, "Carlton Notches No. 20 as Cards Beat Mets, 5-2," *New York Times*, Sept. 29, 1971.

11. Joseph Durso, "Mets Give Up Ryan for Fregosi," *New York Times*, Dec. 11, 1971.

12. Ross Newhan, "Fregosi 'Thrilled' by Trade to Mets," *Los Angeles Times*, Dec. 11, 1971.

13. Newhan, "Nolan Ryan."

14. Ross Newhan, "Angel at Crossroads: Ryan Must Prove He Can Control Fastball," *Los Angeles Times*, Apr. 18, 1972.

15. Ross Newhan, "Homer Lucky Blow, Says Jackson, as A's Top Angels, 6-3," *Los Angeles Times*, May 23, 1972.

16. Ross Newhan, "Weaver's 'Early Birds' Feast on Angels' Ryan, Queen, 12-2," *Los Angeles Times*, Apr. 29, 1972.

17. Ross Newhan, "Ryan: A Hitless Wonder for the 4th Time," *Los Angeles Times*, June 2, 1975; Melvin Durslag, "Ryan Most Exciting of All Pitchers," *Boston Herald*, July 27, 1973; Dick Miller, "19 Whiffs . . . Some Day Ryan May Strike Out 27," *The Sporting News*, Aug. 31, 1974, p. 7; Ron Fimrite, "The Bringer of Heat," *Sports Illustrated*, June 16, 1975, p. 33.

18. Dave Anderson, "For a Change, Another Ryan No-Hitter," *New York Times*, June 3, 1975; Larry Merchant, "Ryan on the Threshold," *New York Post*, June 4, 1975.

19. Pete Axthelm, "Fastest Arm in the West," *Newsweek*, June 16, 1975, p. 56; Dave Anderson, "The Ryan Express Races for the Records," *Sport*, Aug., 1978, p. 69.

20. Ron Rapoport, "Nolan Ryan's Coverup: 1975 was Living Hell," *Los Angeles Times*, Mar. 22, 1976.

21. John Strege, "Old Faithful," *Orange County Register*, June 16, 1992.

22. Larry Keith, "It's Fishing Season for Nolan Ryan," *Sports Illustrated*, Nov. 19, 1979, p. 34.

23. William Barry Furlong, "Baseball's Best Paid Pitcher Comes Home," *Sport*, Apr., 1980, p. 66; Mark Heisler, "Ryan Becomes Texas Millionaire," *Los Angeles Times*, Nov. 20, 1979.

24. Furlong, "Baseball's Best Paid Pitcher," p. 68.

25. Ron Fimrite, "A Great Hand with the Old Cowhide," *Sports Illustrated*, Sept. 29, 1986, p. 84.

26. Mike Littwin, "Nolan Ryan: Fastest (and Richest?) Gun in Alvin," *Los Angeles Times*, Apr. 17, 1980. Ryan's father died when he was a Met and his mother died during his later years with the Astros.

27. Furlong, "Baseball's Best Paid Pitcher"; Jim Kaplan, "For Ryan, It Was a Very Special K," *Sports Illustrated*, May 9, 1983.

28. Fimrite, "A Great Hand," pp. 91, 92.

29. Richard Hoffer, "Armed and Still Dangerous," *Gentlemen's Quarterly*, May, 1988, pp. 292–93.

30. "Ryan's Record Fifth No-Hitter Downs Dodgers, 5-0," *New York Times*, Sept. 27, 1981.

31. Phil Rogers, "The Ranger Rancher," *Dallas Times Herald*, Feb. 19, 1989.

32. Pete Axthelm, "Ryan's Fast-Ball Express," *Newsweek*, July 22, 1985, p. 67.

33. Littwin, "Nolan Ryan."

34. Adam Shoenfeld, "A New Ball Game," *Spirit*, Apr., 1989, p. 41; Hoffer, "Armed," p. 294.

35. Kaplan, "For Ryan," p. 36; Henry Hecht, "Whatever Ryan Does, It Never Quiets Critics," *New York Post*, Apr. 29, 1983; Pete Axthelm, "A Winner in a Lost Season," *Newsweek*, Oct. 12, 1981, p. 82.

36. Henry Hecht, "Nolan's Lifetime Mark Misleading," *New York Post*, Apr. 29, 1983; Hoffer, "Armed," p. 294.

37. Randy Galloway, "Ryan Gives Rangers New Credibility," *Dallas Morning News*, Dec. 8, 1988; Randy Galloway, "Ryan's Smile Gives Rangers Cheerful Look," *Dallas Morning News*, Dec. 15, 1988; Phil Rogers, "Rangers Purchase an Image: Ryan Gives Texas a Touch of Class," *Dallas Times Herald*, Dec. 11, 1988.

38. Mary Flood, "Town Pitches Fit over Losing Ryan," *Houston Post*, Dec. 8, 1988.

39. Quoted in "The Seventh Wonder," *National Sports Review*, 1991, p. 14.

40. Ryan appeared on the cover of *Sports Illustrated* on the issues for May 1, 1989, and April 15, 1991. Bump Wills was the first Ranger player to appear on *SI*'s cover—on March 26, 1977, and then-Ranger manager Billy Martin appeared on *SI*'s cover June 2, 1975.

41. Patricia Baldwin, "Pitch Man," *Dallas Morning News*, July 10, 1990.

42. Frank Luksa, "Feller Misses with Hardball Aimed at Ryan," *Dallas Times Herald*, June 15, 1989. According to Feller's criteria for Hall of Fame induction, thirty-two of the more than fifty already-inducted pitchers would not qualify, including Carl Hubbell (253-154), Bob Lemon (207-128), Lefty Gomez (189-102), Dizzy Dean (150-83), Sandy Koufax (165-87), Don Drysdale (209-166), and Bob Gibson (251-174). Feller (266-162), of course, would meet this standard.

43. Tracy Ringolsby, "Nolan Ryan on . . . ," *Dallas Morning News*, Aug. 23, 1989.

44. "Ryan Gets 300th with Strong Backing: 43-Year-Old Becomes 20th to Accomplish Major-League Feat," Bakersfield *Sun*, Aug. 1, 1990.

45. Joe Gergen, "Ryangers' Star an Icon in the Heart of Texas," *The Sporting News*, Aug. 6, 1990, p. 47.

46. Randy Galloway, "Ryan's Greatness Affirmed," *Dallas Morning News*, Aug. 1, 1990.

47. Why Is This Feller Getting Down on No-Hit Ace Ryan?" *Sacramento Bee*, July 9, 1991.

48. Barry Horn, "Expressly Ryan: In Honor of 300," *Dallas Morning News*, Aug. 2, 1990; David Casstevens, "300th will be Ryan's Reply to His Critics," *Dallas Morning News*, July 25, 1990.

49. Randy Galloway, "Ryan in '93: Last Chance to See Legend Play," Reprinted in *Miami Herald*, Feb. 14, 1993; Gordon Edes, "Ryan Will Leave Texas-Sized Void," *Sun-Sentinel*, Feb. 14, 1993.

50. Tracy Ringolsby, "Rangers Happy Ryan Wears Their Cap as He Makes His Way to Cooperstown," *Rocky Mountain News*, Feb. 14, 1993; Dave Kindred, "Faster than the Eye Can See," *The Sporting News*, Feb. 22, 1993, p. 7.

51. Hal Bodley, "Ryan Record-Breaking Game Ignored by Baseball Brass," *USA Today*, Apr. 29, 1983.

52. Northrop Frye, *Anatomy of Criticism: Four Essays*.

53. A. Bartlett Giamatti, *Take Time for Paradise: Americans and Their Game*, p. 90.

Chapter 2

1. The goal of the study was to provide a behind-the-scenes look at people who work at the ballpark, including ushers, vendors, announcers, security guards, clubhouse personnel, cleanup crews, field crews, sportswriters, television production personnel, parking lot attendants, Stadium Club waitresses, and others. For this study I conducted interviews with and made observations of Texas Ranger personnel constituting over five hundred hours of field work in a variety of settings. For example, on the night of Ryan's 5,000th strikeout, I received a press credential and was granted access to the clubhouse, field, press box, and post-game press conference to study how the 200-plus media representatives covered the event. I also attended some games as a "mere" fan; in those cases, I was a true observer, who interacted informally with nearby fans and workers.

2. Kevin Sherrington, "Critics Give Ryan's Debut Mixed Reviews," *Dallas Morning News*, Apr. 7, 1989.

3. Randy Galloway, "Ryan's Smile Gives Rangers Cheerful Look," *Dallas Morning News*, Dec. 15, 1988.

4. Ryan was on the cover of *Sports Illustrated* on May 1, 1989, and on April 15, 1991; the Rangers graced the the cover of *The Sporting News* on March 6, 1989, July 31, 1989, and August 21, 1989. Ryan was only the second Ranger player to appear on the cover of *Sports Illustrated*.

5. Randy Galloway, "Ryan Gives Rangers New Credibility, *Dallas Morning News*, Dec. 8, 1988.

6. Galloway, "Ryan's Smile."

7. Bo Jackson's home run went 461 feet, the longest home run in Arlington Stadium history.

8. Diane Jennings, "Nolan Ryan," *Dallas Morning News*, March 26, 1989.

9. Fraley, "Nolan Ryan on. . . ."

10. Dean Anderson and Gregory P. Stone, "Sport: A Search for Community," in *Sociology of Sport: Diverse Perspectives*, eds. Susan L. Greendorfer and Andrew Yiannakis, p. 168.

11. Ross Newhan, "Pitching Is Believing: At 45, Nolan Ryan Is a Common Man with a Fastball, the Kind of Athlete Whom Consumers Can Trust," *Los Angeles Times* [Orange County], Mar. 10, 1992.

12. George Lakoff and Mark Johnson, *Metaphors We Live By*, p. 239.

13. Gerry Fraley, "5,000 Strikeouts Rivals 4,256 Hits, 755 Home Runs," *Dallas Morning News*, Aug. 23, 1989.

14. *Fort Worth Star-Telegram*, Aug. 23, 1989; Gerry Fraley, "5,000 Strikeouts."

15. David Fritze, "His Feat Has Fans Stamping at Arlington Stadium," *Dallas Times Herald*, Aug. 23, 1989.

16. *Fort Worth Star-Telegram*, Aug. 23, 1989.

17. Newspaper reports used more clips, but because writers also interviewed Ryan privately (and because they often quote somewhat inaccurately), it is difficult if not impossible to determine the extent to which they used quotes from the actual press conference.

18. Blackie Sherrod, "Our Greatest Cynics Hold Ryan in Awe," *Dallas Morning News*, May 8, 1991.

Chapter 3

1. See Joseph Campbell, *The Hero with a Thousand Faces*.

2. See Orrin E. Klapp, *Heroes, Villains, and Fools*, and Orrin E. Klapp, *Collective Search for Identity*.

3. Daniel J. Boorstin, *The Image: A Guide to Pseudo-Events in America*, p. 49.

4. Klapp, *Collective Search*, p. 18. See also Donald W. Calhoun, *Sport, Culture, and Personality*, p. 330.

5. Henry Fairlie, "Too Rich for Heroes," *Harper's*, Nov., 1978, pp. 36–37.

6. Klapp, *Collective Search*, p. 211.

7. Garry Smith, "The Sports Hero: An Endangered Species," *Quest* 19 (1973): 62; Benjamin Rader, *In Its Own Image*, p. 14.

8. Boorstin, *The Image*, p. 54; Richard Crepeau, "Where Have You Gone Frank Merriwell? The Decline of the American Sports Hero," in *American Sport Culture: The Humanistic Dimensions*, ed. Wiley Lee Umphlett, p. 81.

9. Crepeau, "Where Have You Gone," p. 78.

10. Joseph Wood Krutch, *The Modern Temper*; Smith, "The Sports Hero," p. 69.

11. Boorstin, *The Image*, pp. 48, 61.

12. Crepeau, "Where Have You Gone," pp. 79–80, 81.

13. Gerry Fraley, "5,000 Strikeouts."

14. Tom Boswell, "Ryan Wears Age and Success with Equal Grace," reprinted in *Sacmento Bee*, May 3, 1991.

15. Gerry Fraley, "Texas Rangers," *Athlon Baseball*, Apr., 1993, p. 158.

16. See Tracy Ringolsby, "Climb to 300-Victory Plateau is Getting Steeper as Years Pass," *Dallas Morning News*, Aug. 2, 1990. For example, after the 1991 season, only four active pitchers (Bert Blyleven, Rick Reuschel, Frank Tanana, and Jack Morris) had over 200 wins.

17. Richard Reeves, "Brush with Ryan's Reality Changed View of Baseball," *Houston Post*, Aug. 28, 1989.

18. Klapp, *Heroes*, pp. 27–28.

19. William Leggett, "An Angel Who Makes Turnstiles Sing," *Sports Illustrated*, May 14, 1973, p. 27.

20. Michael Ryan, "'First, Respect Yourself,'" *Parade Magazine*, Apr. 25, 1992, p. 4.

21. Ron Givens, "Throwing Old Gracefully," *Newsweek*, Aug. 28, 1989, p. 65; Todd Brewster, "The Care and Feeding of Baseball's Greatest Arm," *Life*, May, 1989, p. 87.

22. John Shea, "Ryan Celebrates with Bike Workout," *USA Today*, June 13, 1990.

23. Ron Fimrite, "A Great Hand with the Old Cowhide," *Sports Illustrated*, Sept. 29, 1986, p. 87; David Kaplan, "Big Star Sticks to Small Town," *Houston Post*, Feb. 16, 1988.

24. Leigh Montville, "Citizen Ryan," *Sports Illustrated*, Apr. 15, 1991, pp. 128–29.

25. Phil Rogers, "Rangers Lure Ryan from Houston: Team Wins Bidding War over Pitcher," *Dallas Times Herald*, Dec. 8, 1988.

26. Denise Tom, "Nolan Ryan Smokes Only His Pitches," *USA Today*, July 10, 1985.

27. Robert Falkoff, "Alvin Shares Native Son's Achievement," *Houston Post*, Aug. 23, 1989; Mark Maske, "The Two Sides of Ryan Are Both Good," *Sacramento Bee*, Mar. 14, 1992; Todd Brewster, "The Care and Feeding of Baseball's Greatest Arm," *Life*, May, 1989.

28. Ross Newhan, "Ryan: A Hitless Wonder for the 4th Time," *Los Angeles Times*, June 2, 1975; Sam Blair, "Sam Blair's People," *Dallas Morning News*, Apr. 27, 1990.

29. Ira Berkow, "Ryan, Paige, and Rules for Keeping Young," *New York Times*, Mar. 9, 1992.

30. Mickey Herskowitz, "Ryan's Loyalty Isn't the Issue," *Houston Post*, Oct. 28, 1988; Kenny Hand, "Little Incentive for Nolie Here," *Houston Post*, Nov. 17, 1988; Dale Robertson, "Ryan Fiasco Par for Course," *Houston Post*, Dec. 9, 1988.

31. Randy Galloway, "At All Cost, Ryan Must Be Paid to Stay," *Dallas Morning News*, Mar. 29, 1990.

32. Quoted in Ronald H. Carpenter, "Frederick Jackson Turner and the Rhetorical Impact of the Frontier Thesis," *Quarterly Journal of Speech* 63 (1977): 117; Ronald M. Maynard, *The American West on Film*, p. vi.

33. David Kaplan, "Don't Mess with Texans' Sports Heroes," *Houston Post*, May 26, 1989; Skip Bayless, "Need a Hero? Just Send for 'Old Gun' Ryan," *Dallas Times Herald*, July 10, 1989.

34. Dick Kaegel, "Texas Boy Comes Home," *The Sporting News*, Apr. 19, 1980, p. 3.

35. John Strege, "Heat and Humility," *Orange County Register*, June 16, 1992.

36. Bayless, "Need a Hero?"

37. Ed Bark, "An Hour of Nolan's Best Pitches," *Dallas Morning News*, Apr. 1, 1992.

38. Leigh Montville, "Citizen Ryan," p. 124.

39. *Dallas Morning News*, [Editorial], Aug. 23, 1989.

40. *Dallas Morning News*, [Editorial], May 3, 1991.

41. Nolan Ryan and Harvey Frommer, *Throwing Heat: The Autobiography of Nolan Ryan*, pp. 205–207; Dave Anderson, "The Ryan Express Races for the Records," *Sport*, Aug., 1978, p. 71.

42. Herskowitz, "Ryan's Loyalty."

43. Newhan, "Nolan Ryan."

44. Dick Miller, "Ryan Breaks Angelic Peace by Rapping Tanana," *The Sporting News*, Oct. 1, 1977, p. 16.

45. Ringolsby, "Nolan Ryan on. . . ."

46. Dick Miller, "Martin Writes Off Ryan Early," *The Sporting News*, Jan. 14, 1978, p. 41.

47. Strege, "Heat and Humility"; Randy Galloway, "Ryan's Greatness Affirmed," *Dallas Morning News*, July 31, 1990.

48. "To Family, Ryan Is Just a Regular Person," *Orange County Register*, June 16, 1992.

49. Benjamin Rader, "Compensatory Sports Heroes: Ruth, Grange, and Dempsey," *Journal of Popular Culture* 16 (1983): 11.

50. Jim Reeves, "Ryan Is Brightest of Stars," *Fort Worth Star-Telegram*, Aug. 23, 1989.

51. Steve Jacobson, "Nolan Ryan: Whoosh!," *Saturday Evening Post*, June, 1974, p. 15; Tom Verducci, "Sign of the Times," *Sports Illustrated*, May 3, 1993, p. 21.

52. Richard Lipsky, *How We Play the Game: Why Sports Dominate American Life*, p. 117.

Chapter 4

1. Quoted in David Quentin Voigt, "Getting Right with Baseball," in *Cooperstown Symposium on Baseball and the American Culture, 1990*, ed. Alvin L. Hall, p. 33; Sut Jhally, "Cultural Studies and the Sports/Media Complex," in *Media, Sports, and Society*, ed. Lawrence A. Wenner, p. 80.

2. Paul D. Staudohar, *The Sports Industry and Collective Bargaining*, p. 18. As Staudohar elaborated: "The franchise, or right of ownership, itself is a nondepreciable asset. It therefore makes sense to assign a low value to the franchise for tax purposes and a high value to the players' contracts so that depreciation can be maximized." For a discussion of the business of sports and baseball, see also Marvin Miller, *A Whole Different Ball Game: The Inside Story of Baseball's New Deal*, and Paul D. Staudohar and James A. Mangan, eds., *The Business of Professional Sports*.

3. Jhally, pp. 80–81.

4. Ivy McLemore, "Astros Won't Offer Arbitration to Ryan," *Houston Post*, Dec. 3, 1988.

5. Gerry Fraley, "A Ranger He Remains: New Pact Will Keep Ryan, Team Together for Next Dozen Years," *Dallas Morning News*, July 19, 1991; Gerry Fraley, "Performance Key to a Ryan Return: He Will Decide on '93 at Season's End," *Dallas Morning News*, Aug. 18, 1992.

6. Jim Carley, "Astros' Radio Network May Feel Loss of Ryan," *Houston Post*, Dec. 9, 1988.

7. See Barry Horn, "ESPN Strikes Out: Why Show Strawberry Instead of Ryan?" *Dallas Morning News*, May 8, 1991.

8. Larry Keith, "It's Fishing Season for Nolan Ryan," *Sports Illustrated*, Nov. 19, 1979, p. 34; "Is Ryan's Price Tag Too High?" *News-Times*, Nov. 3, 1979.

9. William Barry Furlong, "Baseball's Best Paid Pitcher Comes Home," *Sport*, Apr.,

1980, p. 66; Murray Chass, "Ryan Going to Astros for $4 Million," *New York Times*, Nov. 16, 1979.

10. Hand, "Little Incentive for Nolie Here"; Herskowitz, "Ryan's Loyalty Isn't the Issue."

11. Gerry Fraley, "Ryan's Deal Could Pay $10 Million," *Dallas Morning News*, July 20, 1991. See also Gerry Fraley, "Ryan, 45, Won't Speculate about 1993 Season Just Yet," *Dallas Morning News*, Feb. 7, 1992; Fraley, "Ryan Could Get Out of 10-Year Rangers Deal," *Dallas Morning News*, Feb. 2, 1992.

12. Melvin Durslag, "Ryan Raps Pay Preoccupation," *The Sporting News*, Apr. 24, 1976, p. 23.

13. Galloway, "At All Cost, Ryan Must be Paid to Stay"; Randy Galloway, "Rising Salaries May Hurt All, Ryan Warns," *Dallas Morning News*, Mar. 30, 1992.

14. Pete Axthelm, "Fastest Arm in the West," *Newsweek*, June 16, 1975, p. 59; Durslag, "Ryan Raps Pay Preoccupation," p. 12.

15. Ryan with Jenkins, *Miracle Man*, p. 157.

16. Pat Baldwin, "Pitch Man: Rangers Pitcher Ryan Expected to be Drafted by More Advertisers," *Dallas Morning News*, July 10, 1990.

17. Ibid.; Strege, "Heat and Humility."

18. Baldwin, "Pitch Man."

19. Newhan, "Pitching Is Believing."

20. Ibid.

21. Montville, "Citizen Ryan," p. 124.

22. Ryan with Jenkins, *Miracle Man*, p. 38; Steven H. Lee, "Nolan Ryan Says He'll Fight Insurer's Lawsuit," *Dallas Morning News*, Oct. 6, 1992.

23. Tom Verducci, "Sign of the Times," *Sports Illustrated*, May 3, 1993, p. 18.

24. Michael Precker, "What a Steal! When Bryan Wrzesinski Bought a '68 Nolan Ryan Baseball Card for $12 instead of $1,200, Who Would Have Thought Court Was in the Cards?" *Dallas Morning News*, Apr. 8, 1991.

25. Boorstin, *The Image*, p. 57.

26. "Brine for Nolan Ryan," p. 78.

27. Jack Lang, "Pickle Juice Sweetens Life for Ryan," *The Sporting News*, May 18, 1968, p. 19; Peter Alfano, "Ryan's Struggle to Glory," *New York Times*, May 2, 1983.

28. Walter Bingham, "Say It Again, Rube," *Sports Illustrated*, June 1, 1970, p. 13; Newhan, "Nolan Ryan."

29. Dick Miller, "Ryan's Snake Oil Blessing to Angels," *The Sporting News*, July 8, 1972, p. 20.

30. Dick Miller, "Nippon Slugger, Ryan, May Clash in TV Duel," *The Sporting News*, June 7, 1975, p. 13.

31. Dave Anderson, "The Ryan Express Races for the Records," *Sport*, Aug., 1978, p. 69.

32. Boorstin, *The Image*, p. 66.

33. Ibid., pp. 74–75.

34. Tom Kennedy, "Here's the Pitch for Nolan Statue," *Houston Post*, July 23, 1988; Tom Kennedy, "Did Club Plan All Along to Drop Ryan," *Houston Post*, Dec. 10, 1988.

35. Boorstin, *The Image*, p. 58; Ryan with Jenkins, *Miracle Man*, p. 157.

36. Strege, "Heat and Humility."

37. Norman Corwin, *Trivializing America: The Triumph of Mediocrity*, p. 41.

38. Boorstin, *The Image*, pp. 188, 197; Kenneth Gergen, *The Saturated Self*, p. 57.

39. Boorstin, *The Image,* p. 193.

40. Mike Lopresti, "Texas Ranger Rides Very Tall in the Saddle," *USA Today,* May 3–5, 1991; Randy Galloway, "Ryan's Greatness Affirmed," *Dallas Morning News,* Aug. 1, 1990.

41. Rick Weinberg, "Texas Terrors," *Sport,* May, 1992, p. 42.

42. Gergen, *Saturated Self,* p. 178.

43. Boorstin, *The Image,* p. 187.

44. Ryan with Jenkins, *Miracle Man,* pp. 144–45.

45. Newhan, "Nolan Ryan"; Ryan with Jenkins, *Miracle Man,* pp. 39–40.

46. Fimrite, "The Bringer of the Big Heat," p. 36.

47. Ken Sins, "Life Isn't Easy for Ryan's Son," *San Antonio Light,* Mar. 28, 1992.

48. Frank Luksa, "Fans Have Ryan Signing Autographs at 90 mph, Too," *Dallas Morning News,* Mar. 14, 1992.

Chapter 5

1. Brian Pronger, *The Arena of Masculinity,* p. 15; Lois Bryson, "Sport and the Maintenance of Masculine Hegemony," *Women's Studies International Forum,* 10 (1987): 350.

2. Joe Dubbert, *A Man's Place: Masculinity in Transition,* p. 187.

3. Kimmel, "Baseball and the Reconstitution of American Masculinity," p. 293.

4. Michael A. Messner, "The Meaning of Success: The Athletic Experience and the Development of the Male Identity," in *The Making of Masculinity: The New Men's Studies,* ed. Harry Brod, p. 196.

5. Mark Niason, "Sports and the American Empire," *Radical America,* July–Aug., 1972, p. 115.

6. Hargreaves, "Sport and Hegemony," p. 128. See also Margaret Duncan, "The Symbolic Dimensions of Spectator Sport," *Quest* 35 (1983): 29–36; Michael R. Real, "Super Bowl: Mythic Spectacle," *Journal of Communication* 25 (1975): 31–43; Nick Trujillo and Leah R. Ekdom, "Sportswriting and American Cultural Values: The 1984 Chicago Cubs," *Critical Studies in Mass Communication* 2 (1985): 262–81.

7. R. W. Connell, "An Iron Man: The Body and Some Contradictions of Hegemonic Masculinity," in *Sport, Men, and the Gender Order: Critical Feminist Perspectives,* ed. Michael A. Messner and Donald F. Sabo, p. 94.

8. See Dave Pallone with A. Steinberg, *Beyond the Mask: My Double Life in Baseball;* Hank Aaron with Lonnie Wheeler, *I Had a Hammer: The Hank Aaron Story.*

9. R. W. Connell, *Which Way Is Up? Essays on Sex, Class, and Culture,* p. 28.

10. Ron Fimrite, "Speed Trap for an Angel," *Sports Illustrated,* Sept. 16, 1974, pp. 98, 100; Richard Hoffer, "Armed and Still Dangerous," *Gentlemen's Quarterly,* May, 1988, p. 292.

11. Anderson, "For a Change."

12. Jacobson, "Nolan Ryan: Whoosh!" p. 16.

13. Maske, "The Two Sides of Ryan Are Both Good"; Kenny Hand, "Encore Time for Ol' Nolie," *Houston Post,* Apr. 3, 1988.

14. Cited in David Kaplan, "Nolan Ryan Throws Few Curves in Candid Tale," *Houston Post,* May 29, 1988.

15. Tim Kurkjian, "Inside Baseball," *Sports Illustrated,* May 4, 1992, p. 52.

16. "Ryan Out with a Bang," *New York Times*, Aug. 7, 1992.

17. Gerry Fraley, "Ryan Tossed in 2-0 Loss to Oakland," *Dallas Morning News*, Aug. 7, 1992.

18. Ron Fimrite, "A Great Hand with the Old Cowhide," *Sports Illustrated*, Sept. 29, 1986, p. 92.

19. Gerry Fraley, "Pitching with Pain Not New to Ryan," *Dallas Morning News*, June 16, 1990.

20. Furlong, "Baseball's Best Paid Pitcher Comes Home," p. 68.

21. Newhan, "Fregosi 'Thrilled' by Trade to Mets"; Brewster, "The Care and Feeding of Baseball's Greatest Arm," pp. 86–87; Hoffer, "Armed," p. 292 (Hoffer's feature in *Gentlemen's Quarterly* measured Ryan's arm as 31½ inches from the armpit to the tip of his middle finger.); Hecht, "Whatever Ryan Does, It Never Quiets Critics," *New York Post*, April 29, 1983, p. 102.

22. Gerda Lerner, *The Creation of Patriarchy*, p. 239.

23. Joseph H. Pleck, "American Fathering in Historical Perspective," in *Changing Men: New Directions in Research on Men and Masculinity*, ed. Michael S. Kimmel, p. 93; Lynne Segal, *Slow Motion: Changing Masculinities, Changing Men*, p. 58.

24. Bruce Kidd, "Sports and Masculinity," in *Beyond Patriarchy: Essays by Men on Pleasure, Power, and Change*, ed. Michael Kaufman, p. 255.

25. Jacobson, "Nolan Ryan," p. 124; Rogers, "Rangers Lure Ryan from Houston."

26. Jack Lang, "What Drove Ryan from N.Y.: Concern for Wife Led to Trade-Me-or-I'll-Quit Demand," *New York Daily News*, May 1, 1984.

27. Cathy Harasta, "Married to a Legend, Ruth Ryan Understands Sacrifices," *Dallas Morning News*, Aug. 2, 1990.

28. Bingham, "Say It Again, Rube," p. 13.

29. Peter Alfano, "Ryan's Struggle to Glory: Almost Quit in Met Days," *New York Times*, May 2, 1983; Dick Miller, "Wife Pitching in to Help Ryan Catch Whiff Leaders," *The Sporting News*, Feb. 22, 1975, p. 40.

30. Mickey Herskowitz, "A Ruth-less Spring Training Doesn't Suit Mrs. Ryan," *Houston Post*, Apr. 1, 1990.

31. Montville, "Citizen Ryan," p. 128.

32. Mark Wangrin, "Big Hit: Father Throws Best," *Austin American-Statesman*, April 3, 1991; Michelle T. Johnson, "Dueling Ryans Throw Fans a Curve on Loyalty," *Austin American-Statesman*, Apr. 3, 1991.

33. Axthelm, "Fastest Arm in the West," p. 59; Richard Corliss, "An Old-Timer for All Seasons: For Nolan Ryan, 43, It's No Hits, No Runs—and No Peers," *Time*, June 25, 1990, p. 68; Montville, "Citizen Ryan," p. 127.

34. Michael Kimmel, "The Cult of Masculinity: American Social Character and the Legacy of the Cowboy," in *Beyond Patriarchy*, ed. Michael Kaufman, p. 238.

35. Montville, "Citizen Ryan," p. 124.

36. John Fiske, *Understanding Popular Cultulre*, p. 4.

37. Fimrite, "A Great Hand with the Old Cowhide," p. 92; Montville, "Citizen Ryan," p. 124.

38. Keith, "It's Fishing Season for Nolan Ryan," p. 34; Ray Sasser, "Nolan Ryan on the Hunt: An Outdoorsman with a Touch of Class," *Sacramento Bee*, Dec. 18, 1991.

39. Tom, "Nolan Ryan Smokes Only His Pitches."

40. R. Majors, "Cool Pose: The Proud Signature of Black Survival," *Changing Men: Issues in Gender, Sex, and Politics* 17 (1986): 5–6.

41. "A Day When Crass Gave Way to Class," *The Sporting News*, May 13, 1991, p. 6. See also Hal Bodley, "Ryan: An Oasis from Off-Field Turmoil," *USA Today*, May 3, 1991; Tom Boswell, "Ryan Wears Age and Success with Equal Grace," *Sacramento Bee*, May 3, 1991; Lopresti, "Texas Ranger."

42. Gayle Rubin, "Thinking Sex: Notes for a Radical Theory of the Politics of Sexuality," in *Pleasure and Danger: Exploring Female Sexuality*, ed. C. Vance, p. 280; Gregory M. Herek, "On Heterosexual Masculinity: Some Psychical Consequences of the Social Construction of Gender and Sexuality," in *Changing Men*, ed. Michael S. Kimmel, p. 73.

43. Richard Dyer, "Male Sexuality in the Media," in *The Sexuality of Men*, ed. A. Metcalf and M. Humphries, pp. 29, 31.

44. Thorkil Vanggaard, *Phallos*, p. 56; John Fiske, *Television Culture*, p. 210.

45. Segal, *Slow Motion*, p. 89.

46. Fimrite, "Speed Trap," p. 100; Fimrite, "The Bringer of the Heat," p. 36; Fimrite, "A Great Hand," p. 94.

47. Frank Luksa, "Little Things Make Ryan a Bigger Star," *Dallas Times Herald*, Aug. 22, 1989.

48. Dave Anderson, "The Ryan Express Races for the Records," *Sport*, Aug., 1978, p. 69.

49. See Paul Hoch, *White Hero, Black Beast*.

50. Ryan with Jenkins, *Miracle Man*, p. 19.

51. Barry Horn, "Ryan, Jones, Popular Picks in News Fans' Poll," *Dallas Morning News*, July 7, 1991.

52. Ryan with Jenkins, *Miracle Man*, p. 32.

53. For example, a Nolan Ryan poster was used as a sexual object (actually, as a target) in an article in a gay pornographic magazine. See James Wilde, "The Nephew," *Advocate Men*, May, 1993, p. 35. For a discussion of sports and homosexuality, see Brian Pronger, *The Arena of Masculinity*.

54. Freud suggested that the overcoat can be interpreted as a symbol for a condom. Of course, it seems as though almost anything can be interpreted as a phallic symbol from a Freudian perspective. Sigmund Freud, *The Interpretation of Dreams*, J. Strachey, trans., p. 219.

55. Fiske, *Television Culture*, p. 210.

56. Segal, *Slow Motion*, p. 102.

57. Cited by Bob Greene, "Nolan Ryan Is Newest Star of the Baby Boom Set," *Dallas Morning News*, June 24, 1990.

58. Bryson, "Sport and the Maintenance of Masculine Hegemony," pp. 349, 357.

59. Donald F. Sabo and Robert Runfola, eds., *Jock: Sports and Male Identity*, pp. 334–35.

Conclusion

1. Robin Williams, *American Society: A Sociological Interpretation*; Milton Rokeach, *The Nature of Human Values*.

2. Nixon, *Sport and the American Dream*, p. 10.

3. See Bob Chieger, ed., *Voices of Baseball*, pp. 215–17.

4. Michael Novak, *The Joy of Sports*, p. 59.

5. James Michener, *Sports in America*, pp. 426, 432.

6. Littwin, "Nolan Ryan: Fastest (and Richest?) Gun in Alvin."

7. Hecht, "Whatever Ryan Does, It Never Quiets Critics."

8. Frank Luksa, "25-Year Express: Just Like His Fastball, Ryan's Career Has Been a Blur," *Dallas Morning News*, April 5, 1992.

9. Barry Horn, "Expressly Ryan: In Honor of 300."

10. Fiske, *Television Culture*, p. 210.

11. William A. Sadler, Jr., "Competition out of Bounds: Sport in American Life," in *Sport Sociology*, p. 245.

12. Jean-Marie Brohm, *Sport: A Prison of Measured Time*, p. 57.

13. Arnold Beisser, *The Madness in Sports*, p. 86.

14. Givens, "Throwing Old Gracefully," p. 65; David Casstevens, "Ryan's Routine Never Varies as He Heads Toward Win 300," *Dallas Morning News*, Apr. 21, 1990.

15. Tracy Ringolsby, "Ryan Says Arm, Back Recuperated from Tiring Effort against Yankees," *Dallas Morning News*, July 30, 1990.

16. Luksa, "25-Year Express."

17. Hoffer, "Armed and Still Dangerous," p. 293.

18. John Hargreaves, *Sport, Power and Culture*, p. 134.

19. "Ryan's Present to Teen Catcher: Near No-Hitter," *Sacramento Bee*, July 9, 1991; Frank Luksa, "House's Fall Hardly a Change-Up for Old Hand Ryan," *Dallas Morning News*, Nov. 5, 1992; Frank Luksa, "Ryan Throws Another Curve at Skeptics Who Say He's Slipping," *Dallas Morning News*, July 5, 1992.

20. Phil Rogers, "The Ranger Rancher," *Dallas Times Herald*, Feb. 19, 1989.

21. Murray Chass, "Ryan's Flame Burns Eternal," *New York Times*, Mar. 14, 1988; Strege, "Heat and Humility."

22. Hoffer, "Armed and Still Dangerous," p. 293.

23. Michael Ryan, "'First, Respect Yourself,'" p. 5.

24. Strege, "Heat and Humility."

25. Richard Corliss, "An Old-Timer for All Seasons," *Time*, June 25, 1990, p. 68.

26. Noreen Wales Kruse, "Apologia in Team Sports," *Quarterly Journal of Speech* 67 (1981): 273.

27. Leon H. Warshay, "Baseball in Its Social Context," in *Social Approaches to Sport*, p. 233; Novak, *Joy of Sports*, p. 69.

28. Rogers, "The Ranger Rancher."

29. Randy Galloway, "Ryan Values Team Success above All Else," *Dallas Morning News*, May 28, 1992.

30. William Nack, "Rangers Risin'," *Sports Illustrated*, May 1, 1989, p. 22; Gerry Fraley, "Ryan's Success Rubs Off on Seattle's Johnson," *Dallas Morning News*, Aug. 25, 1992.

31. Dick Miller, "Ryan Breaks Angelic Peace by Rapping Tanana," *The Sporting News*, Oct. 1, 1977, p. 16; Rick Weinberg, "Texas Terror," p. 42.

32. *Miracle Man*, pp. 133–34.

33. George Grella, "Baseball and the American Dream," in *Sport Inside Out*, p. 272.

34. Roger Angell, "The Interior Stadium," in *Sport Inside Out*, p. 156.

35. Ralph Andreano, "The Affluent Baseball Player," in *Games, Sport and Power*, p. 117.

36. Pete Axthelm, "Ryan's Fast-Ball Express," *Newsweek*, July 22, 1985, p. 67; Strege, "Heat and Humility."

37. Tim Carman, "At Home on the Range," *Texas Sports Magazine*, March, 1990, p. 11.

38. Richard Gaughran, "Farmers, Orphans, and Cultists: Pastoral Characters and Themes in Baseball Fiction," in *Cooperstown Symposium on Baseball and the American Culture*, 1989, pp. 200–201.

39. A. Bartlett Giamatti, "The Green Fields of the Mind," in *The Armchair Book of Baseball*, pp. 141–43.

Bibliography

Aaron, Hank, with Lonnie Wheeler. *I Had a Hammer: The Hank Aaron Story*. New York: Harper Collins, 1991.

"A Day When Crass Gave Way to Class." *Sporting News*, May 13, 1991, p. 6.

Alfano, Peter. "Ryan's Struggle to Glory." *New York Times*, May 2, 1983.

Allen, Maury. *Baseball's 100: A Personal Ranking of the Best Players in Baseball History*. New York: A&W Visual Library, 1981.

"Amazing Ryan: At Age 44, Nolan Keeps Performing Miracles" [editorial]. *Dallas Morning News*, May 3, 1991.

Anderson, Dave. "For a Change, Another Ryan No-Hitter." *New York Times*, June 3, 1975.

———. "The Ryan Express Races for the Records." *Sport*, August, 1978, pp. 67–71.

Anderson, Dean F., and Gregory P. Stone. "Sport: A Search for Community." In *Sociology of Sport: Diverse Perspectives*, edited by Susan L. Greendorfer and Andrew Yiannakis. West Point, N.Y.: Leisure Press, 1981.

Andreano, Ralph. "The Affluent Baseball Player." In *Games, Sport, and Power*, edited by Gregory P. Stone, pp. 117–27. New Brunswick, N.J.: Transaction Books, 1972.

Angell, Roger. "The Interior Stadium." Reprinted in *Sport Inside Out*, edited by David L. Vanderwerken and Spencer K. Wertz, pp. 147–56. Fort Worth: Texas Christian University Press, 1985.

Axthelm, Pete. "The Blur." *Newsweek*, June 2, 1975, p. 51.

———. "Fastest Arm in the West." *Newsweek*, June 16, 1975, pp. 56–60.

———. "Ryan's Fast-Ball Express." *Newsweek*, July 22, 1985, p. 67.

———. "A Winner in a Lost Season." *Newsweek*, October 12, 1981, p. 82.

Baldwin, Patricia. "Pitch Man: Rangers Pitcher Ryan Expected to Be Drafted by More Advertisers." *Dallas Morning News*, July 10, 1990.

Bark, Ed. "An Hour of Nolan's Best Pitches." *Dallas Morning News*, April 1, 1992.

Bayless, Skip. "Need a Hero? Just Send for 'Old Gun' Ryan." *Dallas Times Herald*, July 10, 1989.

Berkow, Ira. "Ryan, Paige, and Rules for Keeping Young." *New York Times*, March 9, 1992.

Bingham, Walter. "Say It Again, Rube!" *Sports Illustrated*, June 1, 1970, pp. 10–13.

Blair, Sam. "Sam Blair's People." *Dallas Morning News*, April 27, 1990.

Bodley, Hal. "Ryan: An Oasis from Off-Field Turmoil." *USA Today*, May 3, 1991.

Boorstin, Daniel J. *The Image : A Guide to Pseudo-Events in America*. New York: Atheneum, 1978.

Boswell, Thomas. *How Life Imitates the World Series*. New York: Penguin, 1982.

———. "Ryan Wears Age and Success with Equal Grace." Reprinted in *Sacramento Bee*, May 3, 1991.

Brewster, Todd. "The Care and Feeding of Baseball's Greatest Arm." *Life*, May, 1989, pp. 86–87.

"Brine for Nolan Ryan." *Life*, May 31, 1968, pp. 77–78.

Bryson, Lois. "Sport and the Maintenance of Masculine Hegemony." *Women's Studies International Forum* 10 (1987): 349–60.

Calhoun, Donald W. *Sport, Culture, and Personality*, 2nd ed. Champaign, Ill.: Human Kinetics, 1987.

Campbell, Joseph. *The Hero with a Thousand Faces*. Princeton, N.J.: Princeton University Press, 1948.

Carley, Jim. "Astros' Radio Network May Feel Loss of Ryan." *Houston Post*, December 9, 1988.

Carman, Tim. "Home on the Range." *Texas Sports Magazine*, March, 1990, pp. 8–11.

Carpenter, Ronald H. "Frederick Jackson Turner and the Rhetorical Impact of the Frontier Thesis." *Quarterly Journal of Speech* 63 (1977): 117–29.

Casstevens, David. "Ryan's Routine Never Varies as He Heads toward Win 300." *Dallas Morning News*, April 21, 1990.

———. "300th Will Be Ryan's Reply to His Critics." *Dallas Morning News*, July 25, 1990.

Chass, Murray. "Pepitone Clouts Four-Run Homer." *New York Times*, June 11, 1970.

———. "Ryan Going to Astros for $4 Million." *New York Times*, November 16, 1979.

———. "Ryan's Flame Burns Eternal." *New York Times*, March 14, 1988.

Chieger, Bob, ed. *Voices of Baseball: Quotations on the Summer Game*. New York: New American Library, 1983.

Connell, R. W. "An Iron Man: The Body and Some Contradictions of Hegemonic Masculinity." In *Sport, Men, and the Gender Order: Critical*

Feminist Perspectives, edited by Michael A. Messner and Donald F. Sabo, pp. 83–96. Champaign, Ill.: Human Kinetics, 1990.

————. *Which Way is Up? Essays on Sex, Class, and Culture.* Sydney: George Allen and Unwin, 1983.

Corliss, Richard. "An Old-Timer for All Seasons." *Time*, June 25, 1990, p. 68.

Corwin, Norman. *Trivializing America: The Triumph of Mediocrity.* Secaucus, N.J.: Lyle Stuart, 1986.

Crepeau, Richard C. "Where Have You Gone Frank Merriwell? The Decline of the American Sports Hero." In *American Sport Culture: The Humanistic Dimensions*, edited by Wiley Lee Umphlett, pp. 76–82. Lewisburg: Bucknell University Press, 1985.

Distel, Dave. "383 Strikeouts! Ryan Breaks Koufax' Record." *Los Angeles Times*, September 28, 1973.

Dubbert, Joe. *A Man's Place: Masculinity in Transition.* Englewood Cliffs, N.J.: Prentice-Hall, 1979.

Duncan, Margaret. "The Symbolic Dimensions of Spectator Sport." *Quest* 35 (1983): 29–36.

Durslag, Melvin. "Ryan Most Exciting of All Pitchers." *Boston Herald*, July 27, 1973.

————. "Ryan Raps Pay Preoccupation." *Sporting News*, April 24, 1976, p. 23.

Durso, Joseph. "Mets Down Cubs, 4-0, as Ryan Hurls 3 Hitter and Fans 13." *New York Times*, August 5, 1970.

————. "Mets Give up Ryan for Fregosi." *New York Times*, December 11, 1971.

————. "Pirates Shell Ryan and Rout Mets, 8-1." *New York Times*, July 4, 1968.

Dyer, Richard. "Male Sexuality in the Media." In *The Sexuality of Men*, edited by A. Metcalf and M. Humphries, pp. 28–43. London: Pluto, 1985.

Eastman, Susan Tyler, and Timothy P. Meyer. "Sports Programming: Scheduling, Costs, and Competition." In *Media, Sports, and Society*, edited by Lawrence A. Wenner, pp. 97–119. Newbury Park: Sage, 1989.

Edwards, Harry. *The Sociology of Sport.* Homewood, Ill.: Dorsey, 1973.

Fairlie, Henry. "Too Rich for Heroes." *Harper's*, November, 1978, pp. 36–43, 97–98.

Falkoff, Robert. "Alvin Shares Native Son's Achievement." *Houston Post*, August 23, 1989.

Felser, Larry. *Baseball's Ten Greatest Pitchers.* New York: Scholastic, 1979.

Fimrite, Ron. "The Bringer of the Big Heat." *Sports Illustrated*, June 16, 1975, pp. 33–39.

————. "A Great Hand with the Old Cowhide." *Sports Illustrated*, September 29, 1986, pp. 84–96.

————. "Speed Trap for an Angel." *Sports Illustrated*, September 16, 1974, pp. 98–100.

Fiske, John. *Television Culture*. London: Methuen, 1987.

————. *Understanding Popular Culture*. Boston: Unwin Hyman, 1989.

Flood, Mary. "Town Pitches Fit over Losing Ryan." *Houston Post*, December 8, 1988.

Fowler, Gene. *Center Field Grasses: Poems from Baseball*. Jefferson, N.C.: McFarland, 1991.

Fraley, Gerry. "5,000 Strikeouts Rivals 4,256 Hits, 755 Home Runs." *Dallas Morning News*, August 23, 1989.

————. "Nolan Ryan on. . . ." *Dallas Morning News*, August 2, 1990.

————. "Performance Key to a Ryan Return: He Will Decide on '93 at Season's End." *Dallas Morning News*, August 18, 1992.

————. "Pitching with Pain Not New to Ryan." *Dallas Morning News*, June 16, 1990.

————. "A Ranger He Remains: New Pact Will Keep Ryan, Team Together for Next Dozen Years." *Dallas Morning News*, July 19, 1991.

————. "Ryan Could Get Out of 10-Year Rangers Deal." *Dallas Morning News*, February 2, 1992.

————. "Ryan, 45, Won't Speculate about 1993 Season Just Yet." *Dallas Morning News*, February 7, 1992.

————. "Ryan's Deal Could Pay $10 Million." *Dallas Morning News*, July 20, 1991.

————. "Ryan's Success Rubs Off on Seattle's Johnson." *Dallas Morning News*, August 25, 1992.

————. "Ryan Tossed in 2-0 Loss to Oakland." *Dallas Morning News*, August 7, 1992.

————. "Texas Rangers." *Athlon Baseball*, April, 1993, p. 158.

Freud, Sigmund. *The Interpretation of Dreams*, translated by J. Strachey. 1900; reprinted, New York: Avon, 1965.

Fritze, David. "His Feat Has Fans Stamping at Arlington Stadium." *Dallas Times Herald*, August 23, 1989.

Frye, Northrop. *Anatomy of Criticism: Four Essays*. Princeton, N.J.: Princeton University Press, 1957.

Furlong, William Barry. "Baseball's Best Paid Pitcher Comes Home." *Sport*, April, 1980, pp. 66–70.

Galloway, Randy. "All All Cost, Ryan Must Be Paid to Stay," *Dallas Morning News*, March 29, 1990.

————. "Rising Salaries May Hurt All, Ryan Warns." *Dallas Morning News*, March 30, 1992.

————. "Ryan Gives Rangers New Credibility." *Dallas Morning News*, December 8, 1988.

————. "Ryan's Greatness Affirmed." *Dallas Morning News*, August 1, 1990.

————. "Ryan's Smile Gives Rangers Cheerful Look." *Dallas Morning News*, December 15, 1988.

————. "Ryan Values Team Success above All Else." *Dallas Morning News*, May 28, 1992.

Gaughran, Richard. "Farmers, Orphans, and Cultists: Pastoral Characters and Themes in Baseball Fiction." In *Cooperstown Symposium on Baseball and the American Culture, 1989*, edited by Alvin L. Hall, pp. 186–202. Westport, Conn.: Meckler, 1991.

Gergen, Joe. "Ryangers' Star an Icon in the Heat of Texas." *Sporting News*, August 6, 1990, p. 47.

Gergen, Kenneth. *The Saturated Self*. New York: Basic Books, 1991.

Giamatti, A. Bartlett. "The Green Fields of the Mind." Reprinted in *The Armchair Book of Baseball*, edited by John Thorn, pp. 141–43. New York: Charles Scribner's Sons, 1985.

————. *Take Time for Paradise: Americans and Their Game*. New York: Summit Books, 1989.

Givens, Ron, "Throwing Old Gracefully." *Newsweek*, August 28, 1989, p. 65.

Gravois, John. "Ryan Uses Milestone Moment for Political Pitch." *Houston Post*, July 26, 1990.

Greene, Bob. "Nolan Ryan Is Newest Star of the Baby Boom Set." Reprinted in *Dallas Morning News*, June 24, 1990.

Grella, George. "Baseball and the American Dream." In *Sport Inside Out*, edited by David L. Vanderwerken and Spencer K. Wertz, pp. 267–79. Fort Worth: Texas Christian University, 1985.

Gutman, Bill. *New Breed Heroes in Pro Baseball*. New York: Messner, 1974.

Guttmann, Allen. *Sports Spectators*. New York: Columbia University Press, 1986.

Hand, Kenny. "Encore Time for Ol' Nolie." *Houston Post*, April 3, 1988.

————. "Little Incentive for Nolie Here." *Houston Post*, November 17, 1988.

Harasta, Cathy. "Married to a Legend, Ruth Ryan Understands Sacrifices." *Dallas Morning News*, August 2, 1990.

Hargreaves, John. "Sport and Hegemony: Some Theoretical Problems." In *Sport, Culture, and the Modern State*, edited by Hart Cantelon and Richard Gruneau, pp. 103–40. Toronto: University of Toronto Press, 1982.

————. *Sport, Power and Culture*. New York: St. Martin's, 1986.

Harvin, Al. "Carlton Notches No. 20 as Cards Beat Mets, 5-2." *New York Times*, September 29, 1971.

Hecht, Henry. "Nolan's Lifetime Mark Misleading." *New York Post*, April 29, 1983.

————. "Whatever Ryan Does, It Never Quiets Critics." *New York Post*, April 29, 1983.

Heisler, Mark. "If Angels Want Nolan Ryan Now, They'll Have to Take a Number." *Los Angeles Times*, November 2, 1979.

―――. "Ryan Becomes Texas Millionaire." *Los Angeles Times*, November 20, 1979.

Herek, Gregory M. "On Heterosexual Masculinity: Some Psychical Consequences of the Social Construction of Gender and Sexuality." In *Changing Men*, edited by Michael S. Kimmel, pp. 68–82. Newbury Park, Calif.: Sage, 1987.

Herskowitz, Mickey. "Ryan's Loyalty Isn't the Issue." *Houston Post*, November 17, 1988.

―――. "A Ruth-less Spring Training Doesn't Suit Mrs. Ryan." *Houston Post*, April 1, 1990.

Hoch, Paul. *White Hero, Black Beast*. London: Pluto, 1979.

Hoffer, Richard. "Armed and Still Dangerous." *Gentlemen's Quarterly*, May, 1988, pp. 245–49, 292–94.

Horn, Barry. "ESPN Strikes Out: Why Show Strawberry Instead of Ryan?" *Dallas Morning News*, May 8, 1991.

―――. "Expressly Ryan: In Honor of 300." *Dallas Morning News*, August 2, 1990.

―――. "Ryan, Jones Popular Picks in News Fans' Poll." *Dallas Morning News*, July 7, 1991.

"Is Ryan's Price Tag Too High?" *News-Times*, November 3, 1979.

Jacobson, Steve. "Nolan Ryan: Whoosh!" *Saturday Evening Post*, June, 1974, pp. 14–16, 124.

James, Bill. *The Baseball Book of 1992*. New York: Villard Books, 1992.

―――. *The Bill James Historical Baseball Abstract*. New York: Random House, 1988.

Jennings, Diane. "Nolan Ryan." *Dallas Morning News*, March 26, 1989.

Jhally, Sut. "Cultural Studies and the Sports/Media Complex." In *Media, Sports, and Society*, edited by Lawrence A. Wenner, pp. 70–96. Newbury Park, Calif.: Sage, 1989.

Johnson, Michelle T. "Dueling Ryans Throw Fans a Curve on Loyalty." *Austin American-Statesman*, April 3, 1991.

Johnson, William O. *Super Spectators and the Electric Lilliputians*. Boston: Little Brown, 1971.

"K." *Sports Illustrated*, August 28, 1989, pp. 30–32.

Kaegel, Dick. "Texas Boy Comes Home." *Sporting News*, April 19, 1980, p. 3.

Kaplan, David. "Big Star Sticks to Small Town." *Houston Post*, February 16, 1988.

―――. "Don't Mess with Texans' Sports Heroes." *Houston Post*, May 26, 1989.

―――. "Nolan Ryan Throws Few Curves in Candid Tale." *Houston Post*, May 29, 1988.

Kaplan, Jim. "For Ryan, It Was a Very Special K." *Sports Illustrated*, May 9, 1983, pp. 34–41.

————. "Ryan's Back on the Track." *Sports Illustrated*, September 8, 1975, p. 73.

Kaufman, Michael. *Beyond Patriarchy: Essays by Men on Pleasure, Power, and Change.* Toronto: Oxford University Press, 1987.

Keith, Larry. "It's Fishing Season for Nolan Ryan." *Sports Illustrated*, November 19, 1979, pp. 34–35.

Kennedy, Tom. "Did Club Plan All along to Drop Ryan?" *Houston Post*, December 10, 1988.

————. "Here's the Pitch for Nolan Statue." *Houston Post*, July 23, 1988.

Kidd, Bruce. "Sports and Masculinity." In *Beyond Patriarchy: Essays by Men on Pleasure, Power, and Change*, edited by Michael Kaufman. Toronto: Oxford University Press, 1987.

Kimmel, Michael S. "Baseball and the Reconstitution of American Masculinity." In *Cooperstown Symposium on Baseball and the American Culture, 1989*, edited by Alvin L. Hall, pp. 281–97. Westport, Conn.: Meckler, 1991.

————. "The Cult of Masculinity: American Social Character and the Legacy of the Cowboy." In *Beyond Patriarchy*, edited by Michael Kaufman, pp. 235–49. Toronto: Oxford University Press, 1987.

Klapp, Orrin E. *Collective Search for Identity.* New York: Holt, Rinehart and Winston, 1969.

————. *Heroes, Villains, and Fools.* Englewood Cliffs, N.J.: Prentice-Hall, 1962.

Klatell, David A., and Norman Marcus. *Sports for Sale: Television, Money, and the Fans.* New York: Oxford University Press, 1988.

Koppett, Leonard. "Atlanta Routs Ribant in Taking Third Straight, 8-3." *New York Times*, September 12, 1966.

————. "Ryan, McGraw Are Losers in 9-2 and 6-5 Decisions." *New York Times*, September 19, 1966.

————. "The 'Yout' of America." *New York Times*, September 12, 1969.

Kruse, Noreen Wales. "Apologia in Team Sports." *Quarterly Journal of Speech* 67 (1981): 270–83.

Krutch, Joseph Wood. *The Modern Temper.* New York: Harcourt Brace Jovanovich, 1956.

Kurkjian, Tim. "Inside Baseball ('The Scariest Man in Baseball')." *Sports Illustrated*, May 4, 1992, p. 52.

Lakoff, George, and Mark Johnson. *Metaphors We Live By.* Chicago: University of Chicago Press, 1980.

Lang, Jack. "Pickle Juice Sweetens Life for Ryan." *Sporting News*, May 18, 1968, p. 19.

————. "Ryan–Trade Him or Wait?" *Star Ledger*, March 19, 1971.

————. "Ryan Whiff Saga a Fable? Mets Wonder." *Sporting News*, March 30, 1968, p. 16.

————. "What Drove Ryan from N.Y.: Concern for Wife Led to Trade-Me-or-I'll Quit Demand." *New York Daily News*, May 1, 1984.

Lee, Steven H. "Nolan Ryan Says He'll Fight Insurer's Lawsuit." *Dallas Morning News*, October 6, 1992.

Leggett, William. "An Angel Who Makes Turnstiles Sing." *Sports Illustrated*, May 14, 1973, pp. 26–27.

Lerner, Gerda. *The Creation of Patriarchy*. New York: Oxford University Press, 1986.

Libby, Bill. *Nolan Ryan: Fireballer*. New York: G. P. Putnam's Sons, 1975.

Lipsky, Richard. *How We Play the Game: Why Sports Dominate American Life*. Boston: Beacon, 1981.

———. *Sportsworld: An American Dreamland*. New York: Quadrangle, 1975.

Littwin, Mike. "Nolan Ryan: Fastest (and Richest?) Gun in Alvin." *Los Angeles Times*, April 17, 1980.

Lopresti, Mike. "Texas Ranger Rides Very Tall in the Saddle." *USA Today*, May 3–5, 1991.

Luksa, Frank. "Fans Have Ryan Signing Autographs at 90 mph, Too." *Dallas Morning News*, March 14, 1992.

———. "Feller Misses with Hardball Aimed at Ryan." *Dallas Morning News*, June 15, 1989.

———. "House's Fall Hardly a Change-up for Old Hand Ryan." *Dallas Morning News*, November 5, 1992.

———. "Little Things Make Ryan a Bigger Star." *Dallas Times Herald*, August 22, 1989.

———. "Ryan Throws Another Curve at Skeptics Who Say He's Slipping." *Dallas Morning News*, July 5, 1992.

———. "25-Year Express: Just like His Fastball, Ryan's Career Has Been a Blur." *Dallas Morning News*, April 5, 1992.

McCaffrey, Eugene V., and Roger A. McCaffrey. *Players' Choice: Major League Baseball Players Vote on the All-Time Greats*. New York: Facts on File Publications, 1987.

McLemore, Ivy. "Astros Won't Offer Arbitration to Ryan." *Houston Post*, December 3, 1988.

Majors, R. "Cool Pose: The Proud Signature of Black Survival." *Changing Men: Issues in Gender, Sex, and Politics* 17 (1986): 5–6.

Maske, Mark. "The Two Sides of Ryan Are Both Good." *Sacramento Bee*, March 14, 1992.

Messner, Michael A. "The Meaning of Success: The Athletic Experience and the Development of the Male Identity." In *The Making of Masculinity: The New Men's Studies*, edited by Harry Brod, pp. 193–210. Boston: Unwin, 1987.

———, and Donald F. Sabo, eds. *Sports, Men, and the Gender Order: Critical Feminist Perspectives*. Champaign, Ill.: Human Kinetics, 1990.

Michener, James. *Sports in America*. New York: Random House, 1976.

Miller, Dick. "Martin Writes Off Ryan Early." *Sporting News*, January 14, 1978, p. 41.

———. "19 Whiffs . . . Some Day Ryan May Strike Out 27." *Sporting News*, August 31, 1974, p. 7.

———. "Nippon Slugger, Ryan, May Clash in TV Duel." *Sporting News*, June 7, 1975, p. 13.

———. "Ryan Breaks Angelic Peace by Rapping Tanana." *Sporting News*, October 1, 1977, p. 16.

———. "Ryan Offers an Olive Branch to Martin." *Sporting News*, May 27, 1978, p. 6.

———. "Ryan's No-No Spikes Royals' Protest." *Sporting News*, June 2, 1973, p. 7.

———. "Ryan's Snake Oil Blessing to Angels." *Sporting News*, July 8, 1972, p. 20.

———. "Wife Pitching in to Help Ryan Catch Whiff Leaders." *Sporting News*, February 22, 1975, p. 40.

Miller, James Edward. *The Baseball Business: Pursuing Pennants and Profits in Baltimore.* Chapel Hill, N.C.: University of North Carolina Press, 1990.

Miller, Marvin. *A Whole Different Ball Game: The Inside Story of Baseball's New Deal.* New York: Fireside, 1991.

Montville, Leigh. "Citizen Ryan." *Sports Illustrated*, April 15, 1991, pp. 120–31.

Nack, William. "Rangers Risin'." *Sports Illustrated*, May 1, 1989, pp. 16–23.

Newhan, Ross. "Angel at Crossroads: Ryan Must Prove He Can Control Fastball." *Los Angeles Times*, April 18, 1972.

———. "Fregosi 'Thrilled' by Trade to Mets." *Los Angeles Times*, December 11, 1971.

———. "Homer Lucky Blow, Says Jackson, as A's Top Angels, 6-3." *Los Angeles Times*, May 23, 1972.

———. "Nolan Ryan: Four Years Is Too Long to Be a 'Prospect.'" *Los Angeles Times*, February 28, 1972.

———. "Pitching Is Believing." *Los Angeles Times* [Orange County], March 10, 1992.

———. "Ryan: A Hitless Wonder for the 4th Time." *Los Angeles Times*, June 2, 1975.

———. "Weaver's 'Early Birds' Feast on Angel's Ryan, Queen, 12-2." *Los Angeles Times*, April 29, 1972.

Newman, Bruce. "Hats Off to You, Nolan Ryan." *Sports Illustrated*, July 23, 1979, pp. 12–17.

Niason, Mark. "Sports and the American Empire." *Radical America*, July–August, 1972, pp. 95–120.

Nixon, Howard L. *Sport and the American Dream.* New York: Leisure Press, 1984.

"No-Hit Nolan." *Newsweek*, July 30, 1973, pp. 45, 47.

Novak, Michael. *The Joy of Sports: End Zones, Bases, Baskets, Balls, and the Consecration of the American Spirit.* Lanham, Md.: Hamilton Press, 1988.

Pallone, Dave, with A. Steinberg. *Beyond the Mask: My Double Life in Baseball.* New York: Signet, 1990.

Pleck, Joseph H. "American Fathering in Historical Perspective." In *Changing Men,* edited by Michael S. Kimmel, 83-97. Newbury Park, CA: Sage, 1987.

Precker, Michael. "Baseball Card Fight Ends with Charity: Disputed Ryan Item to Be Auctioned." *Dallas Morning News,* April 23, 1991.

————. "What a Steal! When Bryan Wrzesinski Bought a '68 Nolan Ryan Baseball Card for $12 instead of $1200, Who Would Have Thought Court Was in the Cards?" *Dallas Morning News,* April 8, 1991.

Price, Bob. "Batters Blinded by Smoke – It's Rolling off Ryan's Hummer." *Sporting News,* July 1, 1967, p. 31.

Pronger, Brian. *The Arena of Masculinity: Sports, Homosexuality, and the Meaning of Sex.* New York: St. Martin's Press, 1990.

Rader, Benjamin G. *In Its Own Image: How Television Has Transformed Sports.* New York: Free Press, 1984.

Rapoport, Ron. "Nolan Ryan's Coverup: 1975 Was Living Hell." *Los Angeles Times,* March 22, 1976.

Real, Michael R. "Super Bowl: Mythic Spectacle." *Journal of Communication* 25 (1975): 31–43.

Reeves, Jim. "Ryan Is Brightest of Stars." *Fort Worth Star-Telegram,* August 23, 1989.

Reeves, Richard. "Brush with Ryan's Reality Changed View of Baseball." *Houston Post,* August 28, 1989.

Riess, Steven A. *Touching Base: Professional Baseball and American Culture in the Progressive Era.* Westport, Conn.: Greenwood, 1980.

Ringolsby, Tracy. "Climb to 300-Victory Plateau Is Getting Steeper as Years Pass." *Dallas Morning News,* August 2, 1990.

————. "Express Delivery: Ryan Is a Ranger." *Dallas Morning News,* December 8, 1988.

————. "Nolan Ryan on. . . ." *Dallas Morning News,* August 23, 1989.

Ritter, Lawrence S., and Donald Honig. *The 100 Greatest Baseball Players of All Times.* New York: Crown Publishers, 1981.

Robertson, Dale. "Ryan Fiasco Par for Course." *Houston Post,* December 9, 1988.

Rogers, Phil. "The Ranger Rancher." *Dallas Times Herald,* February 19, 1989.

————. "Rangers Lure Ryan from Houston: Team Wins Bidding War over Pitcher." *Dallas Times Herald,* December 8, 1988.

————. "Rangers Purchase an Image: Ryan Gives Texas a Touch of Class." *Dallas Times Herald,* December 11, 1988.

————. "Ryan's Song: Little Things Mean a Lot." *Sporting News,* August 13, 1990, p. 8.

Rokeach, Milton. *The Nature of Human Values.* New York: Free Press, 1973.

Rubin, Gayle. "Thinking Sex: Notes for a Radical Theory of the Politics of Sexuality." In *Pleasure and Danger: Exploring Female Sexuality*, edited by C. Vance, pp. 267–319. Boston: Routledge & Kegan Paul, 1985.

Ryan, Michael. "'First, Respect Yourself.'" *Parade Magazine*, April 26, 1992, pp. 4–5.

Ryan, Nolan, with Mickey Merskowitz. *Kings of the Hill: An Irreverent Look at the Men on the Mound*. New York: HarperCollins, 1992.

Ryan, Nolan, with Jerry Jenkins. *Miracle Man: Nolan Ryan, the Autobiography*. Dallas: Word Publishing, 1992.

Ryan, Nolan, and Tom House, with Jim Rosenthal. *Nolan Ryan's Pitcher's Bible*. New York: Simon & Schuster, 1991.

Ryan, Nolan, with Bill Libby. *The Other Game*. Waco, Tex.: Word Books, 1977.

Ryan, Nolan, and Joe Torre, with Joel H. Cohen. *Pitching and Hitting*. Englewood Cliffs, N.J.: Prentice-Hall, 1977.

Ryan, Nolan, and Harvey Frommer. *Throwing Heat: The Autobiography of Nolan Ryan*. New York: Doubleday, 1988.

"Ryan Gets 300th with Strong Backing: 43-Year-Old Becomes 20th to Accomplish Major-League Feat." (Bakersfield) *Sun*, August 1, 1990.

"Ryan Out with a Bang." *New York Times*, August 7, 1992.

"Ryan Rookie Card Goes for $5,000." *Sacramento Bee*, June 22, 1991.

"Ryan's Present to Teen Catcher: Near No-Hitter." Reprinted in *Sacramento Bee*, July 9, 1991.

"Ryan's Record Fifth No-Hitter Downs Dodgers, 5-0." *New York Times*, September 27, 1981.

Sabo, Donald F., and Robert Runfola, eds. *Jock: Sports and Male Identity*. Englewood Cliffs, N.J.: Prentice-Hall, 1980.

Sadler, William A., Jr. "Competition Out of Bounds: Sport in American Life." In *Sport Sociology*, edited by Andrew Yiannakis, T. D. McIntyre, Melvin J. Melnick, and Donald P. Hart, pp. 253–61. Dubuque, Iowa: Kendall/Hunt, 1976.

Sasser, Ray. "Nolan Ryan on the Hunt: An Outdoorsman with a Touch of Class." *Sacramento Bee*, December 18, 1991.

Schoenfeld, Adam. "A Whole New Ballgame." *Spirit Magazine*, April, 1989, pp. 38–41, 56–57.

Segal, Lynne. *Slow Motion: Changing Masculinities, Changing Men*. New Brunswick, N.J.: Rutgers University Press, 1990.

"Seventh Wonder, The." *National Sports Review*, 1991, p. 14.

Shea, John. "Ryan Celebrates with Bike Workout." *USA Today*, June 13, 1990.

Sherrington, Kevin. "Critics Give Ryan's Debut Mixed Reviews." *Dallas Morning News*, April 7, 1989.

Sherrod, Blackie. "Our Greatest Cynics Hold Ryan in Awe." *Dallas Morning News*, May 8, 1991.

Sins, Ken. "Life Isn't Easy for Ryan's Son." *San Antonio Light,* March 28, 1992.

Siwoff, Seymour, Steve Hirdt, Tom Hirdt, and Peter Hirdt. *The 1991 Elias Baseball Analyst.* New York: Simon & Schuster, 1991.

Smith, Gary. "The Sports Hero: An Endangered Species?" *Quest* 19 (1973): 59–70.

Smith, Jay H. *Meet the Pitchers.* Mankato, Minn.: Children's Press, 1977.

Staudohar, Paul D. *The Sports Industry and Collective Bargaining.* Ithaca, N.Y.: ILR Press, Cornell University, 1986.

———, and James A. Mangan, eds. *The Business of Professional Sports.* Urbana: University of Illinois Press, 1991.

Strege, John. "Heat and Humility." *Orange County Register,* June 16, 1992.

———. "Old Faithful." *Orange County Register,* June 16, 1992.

Stutz, Terrence. "Bill Naming Road for Ryan OK'd." *Dallas Morning News,* March 27, 1991.

Telander, Rick. "The Written Word: Player-Press Relationships in American Sports." *Sociology of Sport Journal* 1 (1984): 5–6.

"These Are the Mets, Champions All." *New York Times,* October 17, 1969.

Thorn, John, and Pete Palmer. *The Hidden Game of Baseball: A Revolutionary Approach to Baseball and Its Statistics.* Garden City, N.Y.: Doubleday, 1984.

"Throwing Smoke." *Time,* June 2, 1975, pp. 37–38.

"To Family, Ryan Is Just a Regular Person." *Orange County Register,* June 16, 1992.

Tom, Denise. "Nolan Ryan Smokes Only His Pitches." *USA Today,* July 10, 1985.

Trujillo, Nick. "Interpreting (the Work and the Talk of) Baseball: Perspectives on Ballpark Culture." *Western Journal of Communication* 56 (1992): 350–71.

———, and Leah R. Ekdom. "Sportswriting and American Cultural Values: The 1984 Chicago Cubs." *Critical Studies in Mass Communication* 2 (1985): 262–81.

Vanderwerken, David L., and Spencer K. Wertz, eds. *Sport Inside Out.* Fort Worth: Texas Christian University Press, 1985.

Voigt, David Quentin. *America through Baseball.* Chicago: Nelson-Hall, 1976.

———. "Getting Right with Baseball." In *Cooperstown Symposium on Baseball and the American Culture, 1990,* edited by Alvin L. Hall, pp. 23–37. Westport, Conn.: Meckler, 1991.

Wangrin, Mark. "Big Hit: Father Throws Best." *Austin American-Statesman,* April 3, 1991.

Warshay, Leon H. "Baseball in Its Social Context." In *Social Approaches to Sport,* edited by Robert M. Pankin, pp. 225–82. East Brunswick, N.J.: Associated University Presses, 1982.

Weinberg, Rick. "Texas Terrors." *Sport,* May, 1992, pp. 39–43.

Wenner, Lawrence A., ed. *Media, Sports, and Society.* Newbury Park, Calif.: Sage, 1989.

Whitson, David. "Sport in the Social Construction of Masculinity." In *Sport, Men, and the Gender Order*, edited by Michael A. Messner and Donald F. Sabo, pp. 19–30. Champaign, Ill.: Human Kinetics, 1990.

"Why Is This Feller Getting Down on No-Hit Ace Ryan?" *Sacramento Bee*, July 9, 1991.

Wilde, James, "The Nephew." *Advanced Men*, May, 1993, pp. 32–35.

Williams, Robin. *American Society: A Sociological Interpretation*, 3rd ed. New York: Alfred Knopf, 1970.

Wright, Craig R., and Tom House. *The Diamond Appraised.* New York: Fireside, 1989.

Index

The Meaning of Nolan Ryan was composed into type on a Compugraphic digital phototypesetter in ten and one half point Goudy Old Style with one and one half points of spacing between the lines. Permanent Headline was selected for display. The book was designed by Jim Billingsley, typeset by Metricomp, Inc., printed offset by Hart Graphics, Inc., and bound by Universal Bookbinders, Inc. The paper on which this book is printed carries acid-free characteristics for an effective life of at least three hundred years.

TEXAS A&M UNIVERSITY PRESS : COLLEGE STATION